D0284784

C. Alan Ames

Brought to Life

Talks and Interviews
compiled by Beatrix Zureich

1

The decree of the Congregation of the Propagation of the Faith, A.A.S. 58, 1186 (approved by Pope Paul VI on October 14th, 1996) states that the Nihil Obstat and Imprimatur are no longer required on publications that deal with private revelations, provided that they contain nothing contrary to faith and morals.

The publisher recognizes and accepts that the final authority regarding that events described in this book rests with the Holy See of Rome, to whose judgement we willingly submit.

Touch of Heaven (Alan Ames ministry)
PO Box 85
Wembley, 6014
Western Australia

Touch of Heaven (Alan Ames Ministry)
PO Box 200
Kellog,
Minnesota, 55945
United States of America
Phone: 651 565 3027

© Carver Alan Ames - 2003

Table of contents

1	Introduction	4
2	Foreword by Bishop Danylak	6
3	How it all began	10
4	Talk in an African Radio Station	107
5	Talk to the Sick	117
6	Interview	126
7	Questions and Answers	170
8	Invitation or Advice	204

Dedicated to my father Herbert John Doone Ames
R.I.P.   21 August 2002
And
Greta, Hans, Andrea and Eva-Marie Muhlberger

1 Introduction

It was around Christmas 1996, when due to an accident, I had my leg in plaster and started to feel bored, when someone gave me volume one of Alan's book "Through the Eyes of Jesus." This was the beginning of a great change in my life and in my family's life as well. I finally ended up working with Alan's German publisher, translating Alan's books into German. Later on Alan asked me if I wanted to organize his talks in Germany. I never thought I could do that, yet after reluctantly saying yes, God showed it was no problem for Him. Whenever I reached my limits, His Providence took over most successfully.

This is how we started to have Alan come in May each year to Germany, Switzerland and Austria to share the love of God with people, and truly God touched many hearts, healed so many wounded souls and also healed many people physically. We started recording the talks. In each one, there was so much one could learn, and each talk was different, according to what the Holy Spirit wanted Alan to tell those present. Listening to the tapes often, each time I discovered many things that had escaped me before.

Later it became clear that many more people could benefit from the talks if the talks were compiled according to topics and published. For this, we used records of talks and interviews Alan gave in England, Ireland, Germany, Austria, Africa and the United States.

After having it checked by Alan and his spiritual director, we present this little book to anyone who is willing to get to know God more in a new and fascinating way through these words which, inspired by the Holy Spirit, have already brought forth such good fruit, conversions and healings and lead many people to a happy and joyful life in the love of the living God who is Jesus, the Father and the Holy Spirit.

Beatrix Zureich

2   Foreword

Bishop Roman Danylak
Titular Bishop of Nyssa
Canon of St. Mary Major Patriarchal Basilica
Roma Italia

Mary of Magdala, Paul of Tarsus, Augustine of Hippo, Alan Ames. What have they in common? You have read of the first three.

Mary of Magdala, whose name will be remembered wherever the Gospel of Christ is read. Before her encounter with Christ, this sister of Lazarus and Martha, the daughter of devout Israelites, abandoned the faith of her forefathers to search for love and excitement in a pagan Greco-Roman world. Deeply touched by the words of Christ she did battle with the seven demons who possessed her, and reached out to Christ for forgiveness and mercy, as the only one who could fill her heart and release her from the bondage of the seven demons.

The young Saul of Tarsus, lent his witness to the stoning of Saint Stephen, and then in his zeal for what he believed to be the faith of Israel, became the zealous persecutor of those who had followed Christ, until he met Him at the gates of Damascus. Cast down from his blind pride in his encounter with Christ, Jesus sent him as an apostle to the nations and to witness to Christ before the emperor of Rome.

Augustine the son of the saintly Monica, who followed the

6

ways of the Romans and his pagan father, trapped in the blandishments of his common-law wife, found the strength and the grace to give up his mistress and the wisdom of the Greeks to follow the wisdom of the Gospel, to become a bishop and a Father of the Church.

What does Alan Ames have in common with this trinity of saints? His mother was a devout Irish Catholic. He abandoned his Church, his Catholic faith and the Ten Commandments. There wasn't a commandment he hadn't transgressed, except perhaps the fifth; and even with this he confesses that he had almost killed three persons. He met the mercy of God, who sent him first an angel and then Saint Theresa of Avila to save him from the fires of hell and to bring him to a life of virtue.

The steadfast love, compassion and mercy of Christ overcame the reluctance and resistance of Alan to accept the call of grace and love and forgiveness. Christ comes principally not to the just, but to sinners: to the prostitutes and publicans, the drunks, drug addicts, those trapped in the web of Satan's deceit. He leaves the ninety nine in the sheepfold, to find the lost lamb. Like the hound of heaven of Francis Thompson Jesus relentlessly pursues His prey, the immortal souls created by the Father, to bring them to the haven of salvation in His sheepfold.

And when He finds them He sends them to their country folk to give witness of the great deeds He has done, as He did with redeemed demoniac of Gerasenes. Nay more, as with Paul, Mary Magdalene and Augustine, Jesus calls many to become His apostles around the world to give witness to the story not only of their own conversion, but to proclaim the Gospel of Love, Mercy and Redemption to the abandoned children of this world. As He sent his Spirit upon the early church with the charisms of teaching, healing and miracles He calls many in every generation to become apostles and messengers of healing.

He endowed Alan Ames with many of these gifts to confirm the truth of the Gospel in our day and to call the lost sheep to the fold of the Good Shepherd. He has given him the charism of healing. Alan has the blessing and mandate of his bishop in Australia.

This anthology of his selected talks and interviews was selected and edited by Beatrix Zureich, the German translator of his writings and his talks to the German public.

In the simple language of the Gospel, Alan speaks of the truth and reality of God, the Trinity, Our Savior Jesus Christ, the Eucharist and the sacraments, matrimony and the Christian family, the Blessed Mother, co-redemptrix of our salvation, one with the Heart of Jesus in her Immaculate Heart, the Catholic Church, on prayer and the devout life.

He had been raised in these truths from childhood and abandoned them. He rediscovered them when Christ and His Mother sought him out. Jesus sent a guardian angel and then Saint Theresa of Avila to evangelize him. Finally Jesus' Mother veiled him in her love. Jesus had loved Him and pursued him as the lost little lamb and heaped on him grace upon grace, truth upon truth. And like the Church in Corinth of Saint Paul, Jesus has graced Alan with the charisms of prayer for healing and many others, for these our days.

May the Word of Eternal Truth and the Divine Healer continue to bless the work of his faithful servant, to open our hearts and minds to the Love and Grace of the Father and the Son and the Holy Spirit.

Dated at Rome, Basilica of Saint Mary Major
This 25th day of March, 2003, the Year of the Rosary.

+ Roman Danylak

+ Roman Danylak
Titular Bishop of Nyssa

3   How it all began

My mum is from Kerry and she tried to bring me up as a Catholic but at a very early age, I really didn't believe. I thought God was not real. I thought it was a story that maybe a group of wise men had got together and put these guidelines on how we should live without hurting each other and wrapped it up in this story called Jesus. But I couldn't really believe in it… I just couldn't. At a very early age I just fell away from the Church. The only time I went to Church was to steal from it until I got caught by the police and I had to go to court, and that stopped me.

My relationship with God was only one when I was in trouble - I might call upon Him for help if He existed. But really, I didn't believe.

As life went on, I joined a motorcycle gang in London and became very violent and started to drink heavy as I got older. God was the furthest thing from my mind. I lived in the world, lived in myself, seeking money, power and a good time at all times. I didn't realize what I was experiencing was not a good time, as every time I seemed to enjoy myself there was always pain and suffering that came with it, because the enjoyment I was finding was through things of addiction, through sin, through things that were wrong and always there was an emptiness within me, a pain, a hurt, a loneliness.

I migrated to Australia where drinking is very popular, so I fitted in very well. I started to drink very heavily and became an alcoholic and my life revolved around drinking, fighting, stealing, swindling, lying - doing all the sins. I think the only thing I didn't do was commit murder, and I came very close to that several times.

The Voice

One day, when I thought my life was at its worst, a voice started speaking to me. I thought: "That's it, I am absolutely crazy. That's the alcohol. I'm hearing voices now." However, this voice told me it was an angel and that God had sent it to me because He loved me and He wanted my love. Well, I didn't believe in angels, I thought they are like fairies; they don't exist. Yet here was one talking to me. So I suppose like a rational person, I said: "Prove that you are real." So it did. It started to tell me things that would happen in my life. You can imagine how amazed I was when those predictions started to happen. They all came true.

After a while, I built up the courage and told my wife. She was uncertain as to what was happening to me. Then as the things started to happen, she started to believe as well. The angel was with me for some months, encouraging me to love God and to change, but I didn't take any notice. I just carried on as I was because I was so stubborn. I still drank heavy, I still fought people, I still stole and swindled... I just didn't take any notice.

During that time I was travelling a lot for work. One day I was in Adelaide, and it was about half past eight at night, when the angel said: "I am going to have to leave you because you are no different", and then the angel was gone. I felt so sad because it had become a very good friend and I felt a loss. However, very quickly there was a stern, strict female voice which was like an old Victorian school teacher, telling me off. You know, the ones that used to wrap you across the knuckles or clip you around the ear.

 She said she was Saint Teresa of Avila. I had never heard of her. The only saints I knew were Saint Patrick because mum was from Ireland, Saint George because I was born in England and a couple of the apostles I had heard about. Saint Teresa meant absolutely nothing to me. She just seemed to know everything about me and she said to me very directly that I should change my life because if I didn't stop sinning, if I didn't pull myself together, I would spend an eternity in suffering.

She told me that if I didn't change my life, I was going to hell, and that God was giving me this opportunity of salvation and that I should take it because I might not get another one.

She said: "You might die tomorrow or the day after, you don't know, do you? God is reaching out to you now, offering salvation. It is up to you to take this chance."

I think what God did was, at first He sent the angel who was gentle and I didn't listen to it, so now instead, He sent the big guns in with Saint Teresa who gave me a kick up the back side to wake me up by explaining hell to me.

She said I needed to change my life completely to avoid hell. Now I didn't believe in hell. I thought it just was something that had been made up to frighten us into living better. But Saint Teresa explained hell in great detail to me and it really frightened me, it really shook me up. I thought, if this place exists, well, I certainly don't want to go there.

Saint Teresa said if I wanted to avoid hell, I had to start loving God, loving fellow man, not hating them as I did - I hated most people, because I was jealous. I came from a poor family, I saw other people who had money, who had toys, who had holidays, who had things I couldn't have. I became extremely jealous and hateful towards these people.

Saint Teresa told me that I shouldn't feel this way towards other people, because each person is created in the image of God, is created in God's love, that to love God would naturally mean to love other people regardless of how they treated me, regardless of how they behaved towards me.

Surprisingly I found it was so true, as I started to love God all of a sudden I wanted to love everyone else. I remember one day walking around and seeing Jesus in everyone. I couldn't stop smiling and I wanted to embrace everyone, I had to control myself. People must have thought I was crazy, walking around with this big smile.

After having shown me hell, Saint Teresa showed me what could be mine also. She explained Heaven to me in great detail, and I thought: "That is where I want to go!" Saint Teresa said: "You can reach Heaven and anyone can. If you live your Catholic faith, it is a guarantee of Heaven."

Rosary

Saint Teresa said to me I should start to love God, I should start to love fellow man and I should start to pray the rosary. She said to me: "Start praying the rosary fifteen decades a day."

I felt compelled to do what she was asking of me, even though she was very strict, I could feel a deep love and I just wanted to respond to her. But I started to make excuses up, such as, "I haven't got a rosary. I can't remember how to pray it." I had only prayed it maybe once or twice in my life when my mother had forced me to pray the rosary. Saint Theresa said: "There is a shop around the corner that is open and it sells rosaries." I thought: "Yeah, yeah. This time of night. Half past eight. Surely it won't be open." Anyway, off I went and to my surprise the shop was there and… open. She directed me downstairs, and there were loads and loads of rosaries, I couldn't believe it. She directed me to a brown one which later I discovered was the colour of the order she belonged to.

With rosary in hand, I went back to the hotel room but I kept making excuses. Such as, "I can't pray this, so many prayers, so many Hail Mary's and Our Father's, I can't do this!" Up until then I had said maybe 10 seconds or a minute of prayer at night. It was like an insurance policy. If I had died overnight and I had said a prayer, then God would take me to Heaven, or so I thought. That was my sum total of prayers and now I was asked to say the rosary three times a day.

Saint Teresa encouraged me to begin with prayer because she said it was prayer that would open my heart to God and allow His grace to come inside me and touch me. Now I didn't want to pray but she kept insisting that I should. I had a big argument with her about it, because I thought prayer was boring and I didn't want to do it. She kept insisting: "You <u>must</u> begin with prayer because prayer really will open your heart, your very soul to God when you pray in love to Him."

When she said to begin with fifteen decades of the rosary, I didn't really know the rosary, so she explained to me how to pray it. She said that I should see the rosary as a window on the life of God on earth, on the life of Jesus. That when I prayed the rosary, I should place myself beside Jesus and walk with Him through His life. In doing so, placing myself next to Jesus, His grace would reach inside me and touch me in a powerful way.

Saint Teresa said that every time I prayed the rosary that also I should see that it was a chain I was hanging around the neck of satan which would weigh him down and break his grasp on me. That every prayer of the rosary was a step away from evil and a step towards goodness, towards God.

Well, after many arguments I began to pray the rosary. I noticed from the first prayer, I felt a peace, a joy, a happiness, an excitement within, it was truly wonderful. I couldn't stop laughing, I couldn't stop crying, it was amazing. I can tell you that no drugs or alcohol could give you what I was feeling at that moment. I pray that the young people discover this. The more I prayed, the stronger this feeling got and I wanted to pray more and more. All of a sudden, I had prayed fifteen decades, and I wanted to continue.

That was truly miraculous because before that prayer didn't mean anything to me and I didn't experience anything in prayer. Now all of a sudden, it seemed to be so powerful, it seemed to fill me with this joy, this happiness, this love, and I wanted more and more of it and I didn't want to stop praying.

How to pray

I said to Saint Teresa: "Why is this happening? When I had seen other people praying they often looked miserable, they had long faces, as if they were forced to pray. Yet this is really joyful, wonderful stuff. Don't other people experience what I'm experiencing in prayer?"

She said: "Well, often, they don't because so often when they pray, they're thinking about themselves. They're focussing on their lives, their problems, their concerns. When you focus on self, God gets pushed aside. God comes second. When self is first, your heart actually starts to close to God and stops His grace filling you. However, when you focus on God in your prayers, look to Him, look past yourself, look past the world, that's when your very soul will open and God will pour His grace in abundance deep inside."

She explained that's what was happening to me, before I didn't know how to pray but when she taught me to pray, I did what she said. I looked to Jesus and I placed myself beside Him. In doing so, that's what opened my heart because I was focussing on Him but she said, sadly, most people don't do that.

She said I should tell them that when they begin to pray the first thing people should do is turn to the Holy Spirit and say: "Lord, I can't pray properly. I'm weak, I'm human, I'm fragile. I'm easily distracted; taken into thoughts of myself and the world, but You, Lord, lead me past that. Help me to pray properly. Help me to focus on the Father, the Son and You, Holy Spirit, so that my soul can be opened and I can receive the grace that's there for all people in prayer."

She continued, "Once you do that, once you seek God's help in prayer and in all you do, then you'll find that joy filling you, then you may start to experience what a wonderful gift prayer truly is. If prayer is a burden, a chore, a duty, so often it's that way, because prayer is self-centered and not God-centered. Remember in all things God must come first. Look to God in everything and then you'll receive His joy in all you do."

So I encourage everyone to look beyond yourself, beyond the world, look to God in Heaven, calling out to God in every word of every prayer, calling out from deep in your heart that you love Him and that you want His love. When you pray in this way, the way of love, that is when your very soul will open to receive the Divine Spirit of God within, then you will start to experience what prayer is meant to be. It is meant to be a joyful gift of God's love, not a burden, a chore, a duty, but a wonderful exciting gift. If it is not that way, look and see, are you thinking of God in your prayers or of yourself.

Addictions fell away

From the moment I started to pray the powerful prayer of the rosary, evil's grasp on me was weakened. When I started praying and Saint Teresa helped me change, my addictions fell away; and I had many of them. Alcohol was the main one. Anyone who has been addicted to alcohol knows how hard it is to stop. I stopped immediately by the grace of God. This is nothing I did, but God gave me the grace to do that through Saint Teresa. Many of the other addictions that I had fell away as well. Some of them took a little bit longer.

Saint Teresa would say to me: "Every time you feel a desire to do wrong, think of Jesus. Just think of His name, think of Him suffering on the cross or see the Host before you, keep concentrating on that, and you will see your desires just fall away." In the beginning, it was a little bit difficult, but the more I did it, the easier it got and in a few months everything was taken from me. It truly was a wonderful thing, because if you had been addicted to anything, and I was addicted to so much, it really is hard to break that cycle which you are in, because in those moments when you feel so weak, so alone, so hurt, rejected, unloved, you turn to things of addiction, you turn to alcohol, you turn to violence, you turn to many other things as I did.

Now, when I felt this way, I started thinking of Jesus. Instead of feeling lonely, hurt, unwanted, I started feeling loved, cared for. I found I didn't need those things and after all these years, I haven't touched anything and it has been great.

When I prayed focussing on God, all I wanted to do was to be closer and closer to Him and further away from evil. Now every moment was truly exciting. Now I was starting to experience what life was meant to be. It can be the same for each one of you because God loves each one of you as He loves me and what He gives to me, He will give to you. All you have to do is truly seek God in prayer and let your heart be opened in love. Don't be trapped in the world but be set free in the love of God.

Distraction

Often people come to me and say, "You know, it is hard to pray, there are so many distractions." - Well, that is true, there are many distractions, however Saint Teresa said, when you first begin to pray, it is important that you turn to the Holy Spirit and ask Him for the grace, ask Him to guide you and lead you deep into prayer. People say, this is hard to do, and maybe it is, but often it is hard to do because you are trapped in yourself or trapped in the fear of evil.

When Saint Teresa first came to me and taught me to pray, I was in a hotel room in a city called Adelaide in South Australia. While I was kneeling at the side of the bed praying, all of a sudden, the doors and the drawers began to rattle and slam open and closed. The lights began to go on and off in the room. At first, I was frightened, but Saint Teresa said to me: "Don't be afraid of evil. Ignore it. Look to the Father, Son and Holy Spirit and be safe in God." I really struggled as I tried to do that but I found this deep joy I was feeling led me to be able to do this. Within only ten minutes, all these stupid things stopped. I learnt very early on to ignore evil because evil is always trying to get your attention, as when you are looking at evil, you are not looking at God. Sadly today, so many Catholics are afraid and distracted by evil, they shouldn't be, they should be strong and focus on God in all things they do.

Routine

As time went on, though, I got trapped in one routine of thinking of the rosary, and it became a little bit tedious. Even though I was enjoying it, I got trapped in the one thought on Jesus' life. That is all I knew.

Saint Teresa said, there is so much more. There are so many ways to meditate when you pray the rosary. Think of how the Father acted and felt throughout the life of Jesus, or the Holy Spirit, how They shared in His joy, His love, in His suffering, in His pain.

Or Our Blessed Mother Mary, how she saw her son's life unfold before her, what she felt, what she thought. Or the apostles as they followed Jesus, or the women who followed Jesus, or the Jews who opposed Him, or the Roman soldiers who crucified Him. All of a sudden, there were so many ways to meditate on the life of Jesus in the rosary. It has become an absolute joy, it really has.

Later Our Blessed Mother and Jesus and many of the saints were saying to me: "When you pray, ask the Holy Spirit to guide you in your prayers so that you can open your heart, allow God to lead you in your prayers. Don't lead yourself because what happens when you do that, your prayers start becoming repetitious and sometimes they become a routine. You just say them to get through them, and you are just saying your prayers without putting your heart into them, not opening your heart to God and offering Him your love."

They suggested: "Ask the Holy Spirit for the grace, the gift to do this and He will give it to you." So I started to do that and what I found was that with every prayer, with every rosary, with all the other prayers I was saying, I was seeing so much in Jesus' life in different ways. I was seeing God the Father and the Holy Spirit; Their actions in my life. Our Blessed Mother, how much she loved me, so many things were being shown to me which if I had not opened my heart, I would have never seen. However, by the grace of the Holy Spirit, He opened my heart for me and He said: "Tell everyone, because so many people get trapped in their prayers. When they do, when they get trapped in their thoughts in their prayers, getting in that routine, prayer can become boring at times. Then you can start to struggle with your prayers, then you get really hard times where it is so difficult to pray, where it is so easy to give up. Satan magnifies these, he works on those feelings inside so that you will stop praying, as he doesn't want you to pray."

So what you have got to do, instead of turning into yourself and thinking you can pray from your mind, from your heart, without thinking about God, think about God, how He can guide you in your prayers, He can show you how to pray. Say: "Lord, lead me. Show me how to pray properly. Show me how to pray from my heart, to mean my prayers and offer love in every word to You in my prayers," then He will. So many people don't do that. I encourage you to try that and you will find that those times people experience (often called the dry times) when you find it so hard to pray, so difficult, that your prayers get less, these times will become the joy they are supposed to be.

Prayer is a gift of joy, a gift of love to us from God which we should return to God in love, in joy, in happiness. Yet so many people when they pray look so miserable, have long faces. We should be happy in our prayers, cheerful in God's love because God's love is joy.

Catholicism

Saint Teresa also told me that I needed to be in complete obedience to the Catholic Church. When Jesus came to earth, He gave us Catholicism through Peter, the rock, on which He founded the Church. If I wanted to be in complete obedience to God, and trying to live in His complete truth, without error, then I had to live the Catholic way because that's the completeness of God's truth on earth. She explained that if I wanted to have a guarantee of Heaven, that I should live the Catholic faith with total obedience to the Catholic Church because this is the Church God gave to mankind.

She explained that other faiths do have God's truth in them, but not the complete truth. There is always an error to a lesser or greater extent. If I lived in another faith, then I would be living in some way in error. To live the complete truth was to live the Catholic way. The way that Jesus, Our Lord and God, gave to mankind. She said the Catholic way meant to live in the sacraments, in prayer, in Holy Scripture and in a total obedience to what the hierarchy of the Church, the Pope, said - unless it went against faith and morals.

Saint Teresa began to encourage me to go into church more and more. So I would go in there and sit there quietly praying and as I did, I began to see many saints and the three archangels. It began with statues coming to life and speaking to me. I can tell you, it is a big shock if you look at a statue and all of a sudden it becomes alive and is talking to you. Anyway, the saints gave me many messages, but the messages all had the same basic meaning:

If I truly wanted to love God, that I had to live the Catholic way, the Catholic life, that I had to love fellow man and live in the sacraments, in prayer and in Holy Scripture. They said that was the true path to God, the true path which is Jesus. They also said that I must have a total obedience to the Catholic Church.

Obedience

In God's love, obedience is very important, and many of us today find that very hard, as it is so easy to be disobedient when you live in the world. However, obedience means that you obey the commandments, all ten of them. I used to be very selective and say: "I will obey this one, that other one doesn't suit me, so I won't obey that one." The Lord said, this is not the way. Obedience means you obey all of them because if you don't obey in one, you don't obey God. You have to obey all the commandments and you can't make them suit yourself. Obedience means obedience to the Church, to the Pope, to the hierarchy of the Church. Obedience means following what the Church says unless it goes against faith and morals.

Obedience means not complaining, not gossiping about the Church or spreading rumours about the Church and saying bad things that are happening in the Church, because then you are being disobedient. What you should be doing is ignoring these things and many of us don't. We should be praying for the Church to change if it is going a little bit wrong and understand by the grace of the Holy Spirit it will. When there are problems within the Church and when we see these problems, in obedience, we should be praying and asking God that in His mercy, He will help to overcome these problems. We shouldn't be sitting around in little groups complaining and arguing with each other which so often happens today.

Many of us complain about priests we know and think have gone a little bit off track but in obedience to God we wouldn't be doing that because God said we should love everyone including His priests and that we should not say bad things about others or spread rumours about them. What we should be doing is praying for the priests and offering them help. How many of us sit back and complain about them. Many of us say : Isn't he a terrible priest, because he is going down the wrong track, and then do nothing to help him. We don't pray for them, don't offer them advice, offer them help. No wonder the church has problems today. It is our responsibility to make sure these problems do not grow but how many of us accept that responsibility?

Obedience means if the Church says something we don't like, you follow it, even though you don't like it. As long as it doesn't go against faith and morals, we must follow what the Church says. Understand, when the Pope speaks, it is God speaking through him. When the hierarchy of the

Church approves anything, it is approved by God. If you don't agree with what the Church says, you can show God your love by being obedient and understanding that if it is wrong, He will change it and He will put it right because He has the power to do that. Sometimes, however, He allows things to happen so that we can show our obedience, show our love to God, show that we will do what He wants for His Body, the Church.

Many of us today can't do that and I am also guilty of that, at times I see things and I grumble a bit and all of a sudden, the Lord says to me: "Wait a minute, it is the Church, it is My Body, My Holy Spirit guides the Church. When you criticize the Church, you are criticizing Me. When you are criticizing the priests, you are criticizing Me. When you criticize the bishops, the Pope, the cardinals, you are criticizing Me. You are criticizing My Body. Understand what I want from you if there are wrongs in the Church is your total obedience, your total acceptance of My will, a total understanding that I will put right what is wrong in the Church. What I want from you is obedience and prayer and offering of the sacraments so the Church will stay on the right path."

He said that many things put here are tests, are trials for us, to help us grow closer to God, to show the depth of our love to God. So often we don't see that and so often we start complaining, we start gossiping. Then the problems in the Church start to grow. It is when we are disobedient that we have problems in the Church. What a great responsibility we have, because many of us are helping the Church get smaller and smaller by our behaviour instead helping it get larger and larger.

So I encourage you to look at yourselves. See what you are saying about the Church, see what you are saying about the priests. Instead of saying bad things or blowing things up out of proportion, let's start to say good things. Let 's start to pray for them, let's start to support them. If they are going a little bit wrong, let's help them to understand where they are going wrong instead of criticizing them because in God's love, we wouldn't criticize, in God's love we would be obedient to His will and not expect our will to take it's place.

Today, this is so important, because people get tied up in small little technicalities, in things happening in the Church, about whether they should receive Communion on the hand or on the tongue, whether the tabernacle should be at the side or at the centre. They are only little technicalities, but we get so distracted by them. If it's approved of by the Church, we have to be obedient to that, whether we agree with it or not. God calls for total obedience to the Church.

Blind Faith

Today, many people say to me that you shouldn't have a blind faith, that you should question the Church, you should question the faith. Well, I say to people that you should have a total obedience, you should have a blind faith, because when you have that, unless of course it goes against faith or morals - when you have that, then you're placing your trust in the Father, Son and Holy Spirit. As the Catholic Church is the House of the Father, is the Body of Christ and is filled with the Holy Spirit. Where better to put your trust than in God Himself and the

Church He gave us, In doing so, that's when you are truly seeing; it's those who don't do that, who are blind.

Today, sadly, so many Catholics question and question the teachings of the Church and the teaching of Christ Himself. They see nothing wrong with things like divorce, contraception, married priests, homosexuality, and the death penalty. In their confusion and pride, they think they know better than God and better than the Church, and they see nothing wrong in denying God. They see the Church as some sort of democracy - but it's not that, because if the Church becomes a democracy, it becomes man-centered and not God-centered.

The Church is the Body of Christ, the Church is part of God's love for us, it's what draws us into God and makes us part of His body, makes us complete in Him. It cannot be a democracy, but it can be an obedient sign of God's love, as if we love God, we want to be totally obedient to His commandments, to His teachings - that's a sign of love!

When you love someone - your wife or your husband or your children, you want to do whatever you can to make them happy; to please them. You don't want to bring pain or suffering into their life - and surely it should be the same with our love of God. We should want to do everything to please Him and not hurt Him. To please Him is to follow the commandments and to follow the teachings of the Church.

When we don't do that, we offend God, we hurt God and we hurt ourselves. So we must live in the Church, live in an obedient love and not see it as a democracy where we can change things because we don't agree with something.

What is in the Church is God-given, and we must live to that God-given way. We must live <u>with</u> God and not try to change God because that is impossible. When we try to change what God gives us, then we're turning to sin and into the arms of the evil one who laughs at our pride and our selfishness, our self-centeredness, that takes us away from God and into evil's arms which are only full of suffering, of pain, of hatred, of anger. We can see that today in the world, with so many wars, so much starvation, so many problems in the world - caused by our disobedience, our living away from God. If we look back through history, often we have tried to walk away from God, and always it brings us suffering. If only we could walk the path of God, it would bring us peace, joy and happiness.

The call today for Catholics is to live the Catholic way to let everyone see Jesus Christ, Our Lord, in us by living our Eucharistic faith and taking His love with us wherever we go. When Catholics do that, live an obedient faith, a sacramental faith and take the love of Christ with them to everyone they meet, then the light of Christ will shine so brightly in this world, that darkness will flee and paradise will come to earth, but it begins with each one of us living our faith.

If we look to the early church - our forefathers, our ancestors, often they lived in that complete faith and that complete trust in God. Whole families walked out to their death trusting in Christ, Our Lord, and they suffered and died, they shed their blood for Christ, believing totally in Him and afraid of nothing, letting no one take them away from Him and into disobedience.

I wonder how they feel today, looking at the Church and seeing how weak we are, how disobedient we are because we turn away so much and how that must offend those who have died for Christ. We are called to be like they were, totally obedient, totally living for God. When we live that way, just as they did, we will make the Church stronger. So if we live as they did, we will give our children and their children a strong Church and a happy world. However, if we live in the way of the world, we're going to give our children and their children a weak Church and a world full of suffering, full of pain. The choice is ours; we only have to make the right choice, the choice of Jesus, of being Christian, of being Christ-like.

The Call to be different

When Christ came, He called each one of you to be different. He set you aside from the world, to live in His love as an image of His love so that through you, the world could be changed. Sadly so many Catholics today blend in with everyone else. That is not the faith that Jesus gave us. He gave us the faith to stand up and proclaim the good news; the good news of love, of forgiveness, of salvation. The good news of living truthfully and joyfully, completely in obedience to the will of God. In doing so, He allows us to take part in His salvation for the world.

When we live this way, we become Christ to the world and yes, it may be hard, it may be difficult, but it was difficult for Christ. Yes, you will have many crosses to carry, but Christ had His cross to carry. Yes, you may suffer, but Christ Our Lord suffered. Yes, you may have to give your life, but Christ gave His life. If you truly want to be

Christian, Christ-like, then you must be prepared to imitate Him in all things, unto death. This is the faith the early Church had, and this is the faith that many of us have lost.

No wonder the churches are empty, no wonder the world suffers. Today, many Christians, many Catholics say: "The world is a terrible place." Well, it is a terrible place because we allow it to be that way, because we have not stood up strong in Christ Our Lord, proclaiming His good news to the world, allowing the power of His divine and Holy Spirit to flow through us to change others, to change the world.

Many Catholics say: "I am only one person, I can't do anything." Well, in yourself, maybe you are right, perhaps you can't do anything, but in Christ Our Lord and in obedience to His Church, you can do anything. You can move mountains. You can melt hearts. Each one of you can change the world, if you have that total obedience, that total faith, never denying the Church that Christ Our Lord gave us…the Catholic Church.

Another Way to pray

The saints also showed me another way to pray. It was about the sign of the cross because I was just making the sign of the cross not really thinking about it. Saint John of the Cross and many other saints said that this should be a deep spiritual prayer and I should treat it as such. That every time I make the sign of the cross, it shouldn't be just something I did, but that I should see Jesus before me, suffering and dying for me. That every time I make the sign of the cross, I should thank Jesus for what He gave for me. Every time I make the sign of the cross, I should realize how much Jesus loved me. Every time I make the sign of the cross, I should see Jesus with His arms open wide waiting to embrace me on the cross. That every time I make the sign of the cross, I should offer my suffering, my hurt, my pain in life to Jesus as He suffered and died for me. Again, I should be looking to the Father, Son and Holy Spirit, looking to our suffering Lord on the cross, seeing how much He loved me and how much He gave for me and in that sign of the cross also offering myself to Jesus, the Father and the Holy Spirit.

So I started to do that and the sign of the cross became a deeply spiritual prayer for me because now as I started to do it I would see Jesus suffering and dying on the cross. At times, I would see Him tearing His hands off the cross to reach out and embrace me, saying: "Offer Me your pain, your hurt, your suffering."

Doing this, my very soul seemed to open because I would see Jesus, Our Divine Lord, suffering and dying for me and reaching out and lifting me up onto the cross with Him. Always giving me the chance to accept or deny that embrace. I kept begging Him for the strength to accept the embrace and as I did, I found that many crosses were put upon me. Now I offered each one to Jesus every time I made the sign of the cross, and I would feel Him pouring out the grace, the strength I needed to carry every cross in my life. The more difficult life got, the more I turned to Jesus in the sign of the cross and offered Him my suffering and I felt this deep joy, this ecstasy filling me and strengthening me.

I came to understand what the agony and the ecstasy was,

as one day He lifted me onto the cross with Him and my pain was now united in His suffering.

Now by His grace, I experienced His suffering. Not to the full extent because I couldn't bear that, but to some small extent, I experienced, the scourging, the crown of thorns, His wounds and His death. All of a sudden I realized how small my suffering was. When I was lifted on the cross with Jesus, I realized He has carried all of my suffering and everyone else's suffering. I now felt ashamed of myself because I felt so sorry for myself when I was hurt but Jesus said: "That is alright. That is the weakness of your humanity but now that you are on the cross with Me, offer your pain and hurt to Me whenever it comes." So now when I experience pain and often I experience a lot of pain, I turn to Jesus on the cross and offer it to Him. Then I am filled with the deepest of peaces, the strongest of joys and the strength to carry anything.

All of a sudden, I came to understand the ecstasy that Our Lord went through in His suffering. The agony and the ecstasy, because now when I was on the cross with Jesus, I saw that He was looking throughout time at all the people who would be saved by His sacrifice and that brought Him great joy, and now I could feel that joy.

How sad it is today when I see so many people who are sick or dying, and they are filled with a similar self-pity that I used to have and denying themselves the richness of sharing in the joy, in the happiness of Jesus as He suffered. People say: "Was He happy when He suffered?" Well, He was because when He lifted me on the cross, He showed me how happy He was about all the souls who would be saved by His sacrifice.

Now when I offer my suffering to Him, He uses that suffering to pour out grace to others and what He does to me in return is, He fills me with that joy, that happiness that He had on the cross. It can be the same for every one of you who suffers. If you set yourself free in your suffering by offering it to Jesus on the cross, your suffering can become a deeply spiritual prayer which will lift you beyond your pain. It can lift you to a spiritual level you could have never imagined where your very soul will dance with joy, then, like me, you will be thanking God for every moment of suffering.

I discovered that pain is not a punishment, is not a curse from God, but truly can be a wonderful gift when we embrace it in Our Lord on the cross and see how small our suffering is in comparison with His. When you do that, then your suffering, your pain, your hurt can become the deepest of spiritual prayers that can bring you into the suffering heart of Jesus so that you can truly imitate Him in your life.

So from the sign of the cross I discovered, not only is the sign of the cross a deep prayer, but so can my suffering be and it can be the same for each one of you.

Once Our Blessed Mother said to me: "It is when you can thank God for the crosses that you carry, that you show you are worthy to carry them." Now for me the sign of the cross has become a deep prayer and I see so much in it. Every time I make it I try to remember to ask the Holy Spirit to lead me deeper into that sign. The sign of God's love for me and the sign of God's love for everyone. One day the Holy Ghost showed me when I was so worried about things that are happening in the world that if I lived in the sign of Jesus, in the sign of the cross, that I had nothing to fear, because Jesus, Our divine Lord has defeated evil on the cross. So if I carry the cross with me in my life every moment, then evil in my life will be defeated. It is evil that will flee from me. It is evil that will be afraid of me.

Also I was shown that in that sign, the sign of Our divine Lord, that I must become His sign to the world. Today so many people are waiting for signs and wonders, for God to do something spectacular to change the world, to touch souls, but you must become that sign. You must be the sign of Jesus wherever you go. You must be the sign of the cross to the world. When you become that, that is when God will reach out through you and touch others and bring them to Him.

Today, each one of you is called to be the sign of Jesus, the sign of the cross, the sign of our faith. So every time you make that sign, understand what a deep prayer it can be, how it can bring you closer to Jesus and how it can make you His sign to the world.

Mary, our Mother

One day, I returned to England for a holiday to visit my mum and I went to the local church where I used to steal from which is Saint Edmund's in Edmonton. As I was sitting in front of the Sacred Heart statue, it started to shine white and there before me was Our Blessed Mother, so beautiful, so loving. At first, I was a little bit confused because I could see her heart. I thought it was the heart of the Sacred Heart statue but it was a little different, it had some white roses around it. It was only some months later

that for the first time in my life I saw a prayer card of the Immaculate Heart of Mary and I realized I had seen her. I thank God for that because I came to understand I had seen the Immaculate Heart of Mary in the Sacred Heart of Jesus, the two hearts as one.

Our Blessed Mother told me she was my mother and I should call her mother and that she loved me...she just loved me, as I was. That what she wanted to do was take me closer and closer to God, deeper and deeper into the heart of Jesus, the Father and the Holy Spirit. She asked me to call her mother, and I do, I call her mum and she is absolutely wonderful.

She said she loves everyone the same, that we are all her children and she is there longing to help us all, we just need to turn and ask for her help. She reaches out with her hand to take our hand to lead us closer to God through prayer and the sacraments and through the love of fellow man. She said: "That's all I want to do, to bring every person closer to God."

Our Lady said that's the reward that God gives her because she was so obedient to His will in her life that God now graces her by allowing her to bring each one of us closer to Him.

Our Blessed Mother said today there is some confusion in the world. People often say it was Mary that brought them to God, however, she said, understand, always in the first place it is God who brings us to Mary as a reward to her so she can then bring us closer to Him. She reminds me that all grace comes from God and I should never forget that. Yes, it may come through Our Blessed Mother, but everything comes from God and that Our Blessed Mother is a servant of the Lord.

Later, when Jesus spoke to me, he reminded me that Our Blessed Mother is the most special human of all. The fact that she was His mother places her above any human that ever was or ever will be created. That she had to be pure, because God who is pure love where no sin can reside couldn't come to earth through a vessel with the slightest sin on it because then God would have sin on Him and that is impossible. So God created Mary pure, and with her Fiat, with her Yes, she remained that way, immaculate.

Prayer without ceasing

Our Blessed Mother asked me to pray more. She actually said: "Pray, pray, pray." Well, in my logic, I increased my prayer three times. Up to then, I was saying fifteen decades of the rosary a day, now I began to say forty-five, which in the beginning was a little bit difficult, but then, the more I prayed it, the easier it got and the stronger that joy in prayer filled me. So the more I wanted to pray it. However, Our Blessed Mother asked me: "Pray more, pray more!" So I started to say some Our Fathers and Hail Mary's throughout the day.

Then I learnt the Divine Mercy Chaplet - what a beautiful prayer that is, and as I prayed it, I started to see Jesus' sacrifice in a different way. I started to see how much He loved me and the mercy He offered me and every person regardless of who they were.

Again, Our Blessed Mother encouraged me to pray more. In the end, I had to say to her, "Look, I don't know how to pray any more, I'm saying forty-five decades, Divine Mercy Chaplet, all these Hail Mary's and Our Fathers, how can I pray any more? It's impossible!"

She said: "If you offer every second of the day as a prayer of love to God, that's what it becomes. Every thought you have, every word you speak, every action you do, every breath you take, every heartbeat; offer that to God as a prayer of love, and that's what it becomes!"

I said: "Well, I don't think I could do that, that's too much, that's too hard. Maybe a priest, a nun, a holy person can do that, but not someone like me - not Alan Ames."

She said: "Just try, just do your best. That's all that God expects of you, that you do your best. Yes, you will slip up. Yes, you will make mistakes, you will forget to pray, you will forget to love, but just keep trying, keep persevering. Every time you fall down, ask God for the grace to help you get up and keep trying. It's by that perseverance, it's by that trying you show the depth of your love for God." So I tried to do it and it was hard and it still is hard, it's very hard, so often I forget, so often I slip up, but I just keep trying.

What I can say is, the more you try, it seems to get slightly easier. In everything you do, think that you are doing it for Jesus and offering it to Jesus. Every word you speak, speak as if you are speaking it to Jesus or for Jesus. All of a sudden, everything becomes a prayer, everything becomes a joy and you will find you are drawn deeper and deeper into the Lord's heart, closer to His love.

Jesus now says to me that it's a sign of my love that I keep trying and it's the sign of everyone's love that they keep trying. He said: "It's by your perseverance you will be rewarded. It's by your perseverance you'll find the gates of Heaven open to you when you come to your Final Day."

As I did it, my life started to change so much. Before that, every day I used to wake up and think: Oh no, not another day, what am I going to do today? Life wasn't a joy but now, all of a sudden, every day I was waking up and thinking how wonderful it was and just wanting to offer every second to God. Life has become an absolute joy, it truly has, and the more I did it, the more I wanted to do it. I seemed to be drawn closer and closer into God, closer in prayer, closer in the sacraments, deeper into God's heart.

All of a sudden, I was thinking about God all the time and I couldn't believe it, because a few months ago, I didn't think about God at all and now I couldn't stop thinking about Him. Our Blessed Mother was just softly encouraging me all the time, saying: "God loves you and God wants to fill you with His love, and in His love is everything for you."

If you can accept God's love into your heart, your life becomes a joy, and I was seeing that with every moment of my life, and it has continued like that for all these years, absolute joy.

God can use anyone

When after my holiday, I returned to Australia, Jesus began appearing and speaking to me, so I started to have everything checked by my spiritual director appointed by the Archbishop and theologians who began to look at my work as well. They found everything was pure Catholic theology which I couldn't possibly know because I did not learn about religion. I was expelled from school, I hardly knew anything. Again, God shows that He can use any of us simple beings to show His wisdom to the world. When He uses someone like me, it shows He can certainly use someone like you. Don't ever doubt because it is only your doubts that stop God using you as He wants to. Your doubts, your fears and your disbelief. If you have a total belief in Christ Our Lord then He will use each one of you to change the world for the better. He will gift you and grace you so that you can reach your full potential in His love.

Mass

Our Blessed Mother encouraged me to go and see my Archbishop. So I did, and by the grace of God the Archbishop has given me his support. She reminded me everything I did and every Catholic did should be in obedience to the Catholic Church. Our Blessed Mother said, obedience is essential in your faith, that without obedience you truly cannot live your Catholic faith. As I looked to the life of Our Blessed Mother, I saw it was one of total obedience and I wanted to be like her. She said the strength for her obedience came from her being filled with Jesus and the Holy Spirit and the love of the Father and that if I wanted to have the strength to be obedient, I had to be filled with Jesus. So now with many saints, she encouraged me to go to Mass more and more.

I used to go to Mass only once a year at Easter. I also went to Confession at Easter. It was an insurance policy because

I thought when all Catholics die they go to Heaven, so I better be one, that was why I did my once a year duty to remain Catholic. I found that Mass was pretty boring for me at that time because I couldn't see anything in it. It was just a duty, something I was doing. Now I started going once a week, twice a week, three times a week, eventually daily, and when I went to Mass for the first time, I felt this deep love within me. I just felt attracted to the Mass and I wanted to go more and more. I started to be the first one there and the last one to leave, and that was a complete reversal because the once a year that I used to go, I was the last one there and the first one to leave. Now I was doing the reverse and I was really enjoying Mass.

I can remember one of the first times I went, it was as if a hand had taken hold of me and dragged me into the church. There was this pulling, a magnetism inside me; then, as I came into the church, I was filled with joy, with happiness, with this excitement I was feeling in prayer, but a hundred times stronger, a thousand times stronger. It was almost complete ecstasy.

As the priest Fr. Sean Sorehan started to say Mass, his words seemed to come alive in the air before me and seemed to surround me and pull me into them and fill me with something like electricity. I started to realize each word was a prayer to the Father, the Son and the Holy Spirit. I wanted to be part of these prayers. I wanted to praise and worship God, to adore God and express my love for God in each word the priest was saying. I wanted to unite with the priest in love of God in a special way in the Eucharist. Now I realized that every word of the Eucharist was sacred, was holy, was precious. I realized that in each of those words was the power and the love of the Holy Spirit, and I could feel that power and love filling me and lifting me higher and higher in this ecstasy. I felt like I would just burst open and die and I would have been happy to.

As I looked to the priest at the altar, he changed to be Jesus with the apostles around him. I saw the Last Supper, the sacrifice of Jesus, the resurrection and so much more. I was at the Last Supper with Jesus. Then later, I saw every Mass that ever happened, and that when I received the Eucharist, that I was part of every Mass that ever happened. I could see in the Host Jesus reaching out to me to embrace me and fill me with His love. In the Host, I saw the face of Jesus. At times, when the Host was broken in half, it would start to bleed and the blood would flow towards me and surround me and fill me with the deepest of peace I have ever known, with security, with love. Now the Mass was truly coming to life and I never wanted it to end.

Then I went to Communion, and as I was going up to receive the Lord, my heart was beating faster and faster. I had this ache inside to receive Communion; I longed for it, and then, when I received Jesus, I was overwhelmed with the greatest of loves, lifted beyond this world into the deepest joy you could ever imagine. Truly I had a touch of Heaven in my heart and I wondered why I had never been to Mass before and experienced this. For nine years now, every time I go to Communion, I experience that to a greater or lesser extent.

Now the Eucharist has become the centre of my life. Every day, I long, I yearn for the Eucharist. I can't wait to receive

Jesus within. Sometimes, when I come into church I feel like falling onto my knees and calling out: Lord, I love You and I want You within me. When I am travelling and I am on a plane and I can't go to Mass, sometimes I break down and cry. Yes, I can have a spiritual union, but I can't have that physical union with Jesus Our Divine Lord, and there is something missing within me.

Later I said to Jesus: "Why was this happening? In the past, the Mass meant little to me, but now, I cannot keep away."

He answered: "Well, before, you were blind to the truth but as you started to pray, that blindness was being taken away because when you're reaching out in love to Me in prayer, that blindness is being lifted from you and then you start to see the truth. The truth is that I am present in every Eucharist. I am there, reaching out to each person to say I love them and that I care for them. Now you have started to celebrate the Eucharist as you should, now that you are reaching out to Me and saying that you love Me, that you care for Me, that you want My love."

This was true because every time I go to Mass now, I have this longing and ache inside me. I feel like falling on my knees and begging God to touch Me and fill me with His love, because it's so sweet, so pure, so wonderful.

It should be the same for everyone. In every Mass you must come seeking God, longing for God, aching for God. In every Mass you must come seeking the kingdom of God. The Lord said, when you come in that way, the way of love, then your heart and very soul will open so that you can receive Him the way you should. Then you will start to experience the Eucharist as you should. You will start to experience the overwhelming love of God filling your soul. When you come and bow down humbly before God and ask Him to fill you with His love, He will.

I guarantee you that once you experience that you will never want to be away from the Mass because nothing in this world compares to it. The joy, the happiness, the ecstasy is beyond our understanding. He said that can be the same for everyone because He loves you as He loves me and He wants to give you what He gives to me. All He asks is that you come and give yourself to Him in the Eucharist.

The Lord said again, "Now you're celebrating the Mass as you should." He continued, "It's so sad that today, most people don't celebrate the Eucharist as they should." Even the devout, because when they come to Mass, so often they're focused on themselves and their lives. Sometimes they wonder isn't the priest's homily going on so long, I wish it would finish, I am in a hurry, I have things to do after Mass. They start thinking about their job, their family, their friends, anything but the Mass, anything but God, so often distracted into thoughts of self.

The Lord explained, "When self is first, God is second." That barrier of self comes up again, and you can't receive the Lord within as you should, because you're putting yourself first instead of God.

He said, "Many people do not understand that the Eucharist is the greatest gift I give to mankind." This is where God lowers Himself so that He can come into us so that for a moment we can be one with divinity.

Again, you must look beyond yourself and look to God. When you come to the Eucharist you must be seeking

God's love, seeking to be one in His love. You should have that ache within you, that desire to receive Jesus. When you come in this way, that is when your heart and soul will open so you can receive Him as you should, receive Him in the way of love. He said, "Sadly, most people don't do that and then they miss out on so much in the Eucharist."

I responded, "But it's hard for people. I've been shown the wonder of the Eucharist, but most people have not. How do they overcome these distractions, as there's so much to distract them in life?"

The Lord explained that people have to recognize how weak they are, how fragile they are, how human they are. Then what they have to do is turn to the Holy Spirit before the Mass starts and say, "Here I am, Lord, a weak, fragile human. By myself, it is impossible for me to celebrate this divine mystery in the way I should but You Lord, You take my very soul and lead me past myself, into Your love."

Once you come before God in this humble way, recognizing how weak you are and asking for His strength, His guidance, He will take you by the hand and lead you deep into the mystery of the Eucharist which is so wonderful.

He continued to explain, "When you come to Mass, you should focus entirely on Me. Spend that time with Me, alone with Me, focus on Me in the Eucharist. When you do, the Mass will come alive for you, and I will reach out to you and fill you with My love, My joy. I will lift all your pain, all your suffering, all your hurts, all your loneliness and replace it with My love."

It was explained that in the Eucharist, God lowers Himself to come into each one of us. That He allows us to be one with God, for a moment united with divinity, to have a touch of Heaven in our very soul. If people truly understood what was offered to them, the churches would be packed and there would be queues miles long to receive Communion. However, if the devout do not live the Eucharist, how can they expect anyone else to come to it?

The Lord said you must focus on Him, on the Father, the Son and the Holy Spirit. You must give yourself completely to God in the Eucharist as He gives Himself to you.

So many people come to the Mass to receive Jesus, and of course, that is the greatest gift, but in that receiving, you must be prepared to give yourself to Him. You must come and say, "Here I am, Lord, I come to do Your will, I come to serve You." When you come and say that and mean that, then Jesus will pour out His Holy Spirit in abundance into your life, and then it will be your duty as it is in every Mass, not to keep Jesus to yourself, but to take Him out the church door to everyone you meet. Jesus calls every one of us to take Him to the whole world. That is a duty, a duty sadly many Catholics do not fulfil.

The Lord said that the Eucharist is the greatest treasure He gives to mankind today.

The Lord said to me, "The Eucharist is the greatest prayer of all," and that people don't understand that in the Eucharist, it is the Lord Himself, it is divinity Himself coming to us to fill us with Him, if we take away all barriers, all doubts, all disbelief. He will fill us entirely with

His love and make our life complete in Him. He explained that the Eucharist is the greatest gift God gives to mankind today, yet so many people cannot believe and so many people who do believe come along and don't take part as they should. They are just there.

He continued to explain, "Every time you come to the Eucharist, make yourself one with Me by accepting Me totally within and focussing on Me and allowing Me to give you all the gifts, all the graces that I want to through the Eucharist. Make the Eucharist the centre of your life, and then you will start to live." All of a sudden, by His grace, I did. Now every day was becoming a joy instead of a misery. The Eucharist truly is the greatest healing prayer of all. All we have to do is accept it and believe.

Mass is a Trinitarian Celebration

So many people when they come to the Eucharist forget that it is a Trinitarian celebration with the Father, the Son and the Holy Spirit. Not only Jesus, but the Father and the Holy Spirit are there. Many of the prayers of the Holy Mass are to the Father but how often do we think about the Father in the Mass?

Again, so often we're thinking about ourselves, and maybe we're having an occasional thought about Jesus, but how often do we think about the Father? The Father who gives us this wonderful gift in His Son by the power of His Spirit. The Father who offers us so much and reaches out to us in the Eucharist and says, "Yes, I am your Father, yes, you are My children, and here I'm offering you the food you need to live; the food of life. When you accept Me as your Father, when you accept what I offer you, then you can start to live as you should, live a complete, a holy life." It takes you accepting being part of the family of God, accepting the Father, the Son and the Holy Spirit and what God asks of you.

The Mass truly is a Trinitarian celebration of love where we offer prayers and the sacrifice of Jesus to the Father in Heaven by the power of the Holy Spirit and we can be drawn deep into this Trinitarian love when we truly seek God in every moment of the Eucharist. When we look beyond ourselves, beyond the world.

When you start to live the Eucharist in that way, it changes your life completely. If you think your faith is strong now, wait until you start to live every Eucharist as you should because now in yourself, in your humanity, you start to feel so weak before the greatness of God and in the greatness of God. Now you realize that once you receive Jesus in the Eucharist, that you are filled with the power of God, the power of Heaven, and that you are strong. That you are strong in the graces, in the gifts, in the love of God and that is when you understand you can do anything because God is truly with you and you are truly with Him. This is when you can truly call yourself Christian because then you become Christ-like and then your life changes.

Before I was eucharistic, I felt so unloved, so unwanted, so uncared for; less than others. Now in our eucharistic Lord Jesus Christ, I know I am loved, I know I am wanted because Jesus is with me, caring for me, protecting me, looking after me, loving me. Now I know in God's eyes, like everyone else, I am a treasure.

Jesus said, "Unless you eat and drink of My body and of My blood, you shall not have life within you,' and Saint Paul said, you must do that worthily. To be worthy, apart from living a good life, you must come to the Eucharist, seeking God, focussing on God and then you will come to true life. Then everything will become clear to you. You will not have fear in your life. Sometimes I go to the most dangerous places in the world, and I am not afraid because I know now God is with me and nothing can happen to me unless God allows it to happen. This is how every Catholic should be, knowing that in Our eucharistic Lord God Jesus Christ, you are safe.

So many Catholics today are worried about the end times, about the anti-Christ, about satan himself but please understand that the weakest one of you, the most fragile one of you, filled with Jesus Christ in the Eucharist, totally believing in Our Eucharistic Lord God, and totally obedient to His will, is stronger than satan himself! I tell you if satan was to walk in here right now and anyone of you was living strongly in the Eucharist, he would flee in terror. That is the power of Our God in the Eucharist. Jesus is the victor, He has won and in Jesus in the Eucharist we too become the victors!

How sad it is that so many Catholics walk around as if we are the defeated. If you hold on to the Eucharistic love of God, if you cling to the cross of victory, walk unafraid wherever you go, then that victory will flow through you to change the world. Each one of you can be a powerhouse of goodness, a powerhouse of God. You only have to make your fiat as Mary did. In every Eucharist, if you say your yes, and when the Mass is over, go out the church door taking Jesus to everyone you meet, then one day this world will be paradise again. When a billion Catholics start to live this Eucharistic faith, the world will be overwhelmed with the love and grace of God.

I tell you in all truth that no one and nothing can stand against that and it is your duty to live that way. When you do not, you are denying your God and you are denying yourself.

The Healing in the Mass

The Mass is the greatest healing prayer. Jesus said that there are so many sick today and they often go anywhere for healing, except to God. He said that in the Eucharist, God will heal you. We say in the Eucharist, "Only say the word, Lord, and I shall be healed,' but how many of us believe that? We say it and we don't even think what we are saying. Jesus is saying that word in every Eucharist, "Be healed. I love you, I want to heal you and I want you to accept My healing."

In the Eucharist, Jesus comes into you, He brings His healing love, His healing light, Himself to you. When He comes in, all your pain, your suffering, your hurt can just fall away. All these feelings of being unloved, unwanted, uncared for, so lonely... will all fall away, for now you are secure in the love of God and no matter what happens in your life, nothing can hurt you because now you know you have Jesus with you and He loves you, He cares for you, and He wants to protect you.

Many Catholics go to doctors and sometimes don't get healed. They may even go to new age people to get healed but how many truly come to the Eucharist seeking healing?

Here in the Eucharist is the greatest physician of all, Jesus Himself. He can heal anything and if you believed, you would be healed in the way that is best for you; spiritually, physically or emotionally.

The Eucharist is the centre of our faith. We must live the Eucharist, we must believe in the Eucharist and we must place ourselves in the Eucharist as often as we can.

So many people say they love Jesus and they go to Mass on Sunday. Or maybe twice a week or three times a week but you know, if you love your husband or your wife or your children, don't you want to see them every day? Don't you want to be with them every day? Surely it should be the same with Jesus. If you love Him, you would want to be with Him in the Eucharist every day. There are so many excuses not to be that way but really, there are very few good reasons.

The real Divine Presence in the Eucharist

I did not believe that the bread and wine were the Body and Blood of Jesus. I thought it was a symbolic act. I thought the apostles did it, so we did it to carry on the tradition.

One day, Jesus said to me, "I have got the gift of a smile for you," and I thought, everyone could smile. I thought: what sort of gift is that? The next day, when I went to Mass, and I received Communion, I was in absolute ecstasy. I could not stop smiling, it was wonderful. There was tears rolling down my cheeks, and I started to feel embarrassed, and I thought people were looking at me. So I tried to stop smiling, and the more I tried to stop, the more I smiled, it was incredible. Since then, every time I receive Communion, I am filled to a greater or lesser extent with ecstasy.

Over the weeks, as my wife was coming to Mass with me, she was getting embarrassed and started nudging me in the side saying, "Stop it, stop it," I just can't as I am filled with the love of God when the Lord shows me every day that it truly is His Body and Blood in the bread and the wine. What I had forgotten is that God created the universe, He created you and me, He created everything and if He wants to change bread and wine into His Body and Blood, then He can do it. He has the power and He has shown this to me many times.

Once I was going to a 'Life in the Spirit' seminar and I was praying with people and the Sacrament was exposed, and as I turned and looked at the Sacrament, the face of Jesus was there. So I turned back and carried on praying, and I didn't say anything to the people. Then they all started to rush forward, kneeling down before the Sacrament, and they could all see Jesus in the Host and Mary beside it and when I turned back and looked, Our Lady was there as well with a beautiful golden halo.

Just a few months ago, my wife saw Jesus in the Sacrament one night when she was filled with the Spirit, and just last week in Ireland, she saw Our Blessed Mother in front of the Sacrament. Nearly every day, I see the face of Jesus in the Host. It truly is Jesus, He proves it to me over and over and to so many other people because a couple of times I said to Him, "It is only me seeing this." So He started to show it to other people, and they often come to me saying they have seen Him in the Sacrament and that they now believe He truly is in the bread and wine. It truly is His Body and Blood.

I was giving a talk in Hanwell, London and my sister-in-law came along who is not even baptised. The Host was exposed for the healing prayers. Afterwards, she said to my brother: "There was a beautiful picture of Jesus on the altar." He asked, "What picture?" She said: "On that white thing that was up on the altar, it had Jesus in it," and she was talking about the Host. Here was someone who was not even baptised, seeing Jesus in the Host and the Lord was showing her, it truly is His Body and Blood.

I see this so often and many other people say this to me now, it is happening more and more. This is the Lord saying, it truly is His Body and Blood, believe, believe, because it is true.

However, sometimes what happens is, the evil one is there putting doubts in our mind, saying, "Do not believe, it is only bread and wine!" Why is he doing that? Because God is offering us so much in the Eucharist, He is offering us everything, Himself. In the Eucharist, we can get all we need in this life to come closer to God to live our lives complete in God's love. No wonder satan attacks us with doubts, with disbelief. What Jesus said to me was, "In these times, when you are getting these doubts, when you think maybe it is not Me, just think of My name, think of My passion and you will see these doubts just fade away." So I started to do that, and they did, they just disappeared, and now nearly every day I see Jesus in the Host, and when I receive Him within, He fills me with ecstasy, fills me with love. He explained, "This is happening because you truly believe." Also He confirmed that this is there for everyone, this love, this joy, if only they open their hearts and believe it truly is His Body and Blood.

Priests

When one day I saw the priest changing before me in the Mass to become Jesus, the Lord explained to me that the priest should be Jesus to me and to everyone. Every time I see a priest I also should see Jesus standing there reaching out to me in love. How sad it is today that many people don't see that. So often people gossip about priests and say bad things about them. So often people are using priests for the sacraments, for Mass, marriage, confession, baptism, and when they are in trouble, they come, seeking help from the priest. So we use the priests instead of loving them as part of our family.

In every priest we should see Christ before us and we should see the sacrifice that each priest has made to serve God and to serve others. We should respect them and thank them for that. Sometimes when priests slip up or make mistakes, which happens because they are human like you and me, we shouldn't be condemning and judging, we should be reaching out to help them and love them just as we expect them to do to us. So many people today complain about the problems they have in their families with their husband or wife, with their children or uncles and aunts and they ask, "What can we do to overcome this, what can we do to live a better life in our families?" The answer should be obvious: Bring the priests to become part of your family. Bring them for dinner, for lunch, for coffee, for tea. When you do this, the love of God will shine so strongly through the priests and touch your families and it will help bring peace and counteract all the bad influences that are put upon families today. The presence of the priest will strengthen your family and help bring it back to God.

Today so many people forget the priests and forget how holy, how sacred, how special they are and how important they are to us. So many people come to me for healing but how many of them go to a priest and ask for a healing prayer or for a blessing? The priests have the most powerful hands of all because it is by the grace of God that priests and priests alone can change the bread and wine into the Body and Blood of Jesus. No other hands can do that! What power they have in their hands, the power of God. Yet so often, we forget them.

Visions of Saints

Angels and saints started appearing to me and I have seen many different saints, many angels. I see them sitting in the church or walking in the streets, everywhere. I remember one day going to church, and I kept seeing this old man who would be sitting there. He would never speak to me, and I just thought he was a normal person like you or me. I didn't know who he was. I would be praying or just sitting there contemplating and he was just there and I was aware of his presence. I went into another church some time later and I saw a card on the side that had a photo of this man on it and I picked it up, and it said it was Padre Pio. This was the first time I had seen his picture. I had been seeing him for a long time but I never knew who he was and there has been many things happening like that. I didn't know who I was seeing, and later on I discovered who it was I was seeing!

One day Saint Stephen, Saint Matthew and Saint Andrew started speaking to me. I have said many times, I couldn't understand why it was me, I kept saying: "Why me? There are so many good people who come to church because they love God, so many religious people, yet you are talking to me who has been so bad, who is so bad." They explained, "It is because God loves you and He loves you the same as anyone else, the only difference is how much you love God. Also it shows that by God appearing to you, someone who was so far away from Him, that His love is there for everyone, even the worst sinner, not just a select few."

Saint Stephen was very special to me and I grew very fond of him, he has become one of my favourite saints. He showed me, how at the time of his death, when the people were stoning him and killing him, that he forgave them and how he prayed to Jesus for their forgiveness and how the Lord came and led him to Heaven. He showed me at that time something very special, because I used to get so angry with people. It was very easy for me to get into a fight, or fall into an argument with someone.

Now Saint Stephen was showing me that no matter how people abused you, no matter how they treated you, you should just show them love, always love. He showed me that if you give out love, you get love back. That if you give out hate that is what you get back. All of a sudden, I was seeing things differently, and I was not getting angry too much. Instead of hating people, I was trying to love them. I was seeing that if Saint Stephen could do it at his death, then maybe I could do it at the difficult moments I had. People who used to be my enemies, all of a sudden were becoming my friends. Life was changing, and it was absolutely wonderful.

Marriage

The other thing Saint Stephen was talking about was how important marriage was. I mean I loved my wife, or I thought I did at that time, but we used to have lots of arguments, as many married people do. I caused my wife many problems over the years. I think it is only by the grace of God that she stayed with me. I never appreciated what marriage really was but Saint Stephen began to explain it to me. He said that marriage is a holy sacrament, that in marriage you make a promise before God to love each other, no matter what happens, no matter the difficulties. That I should see that marriage is a Trinitarian celebration of love with God as the head of the marriage and my wife and myself immersed in His love. It is a gift from God to us which we return to God every day after we have taken our vows before Him, made our vows of love before the Lord. He said that I should remember that God watches over my marriage every second and He treasured the moments of love in our marriage. Each day, God looks upon our marriage and treasures the gift that we return to Him, the gift of love. He looks at the joy and the happiness in each marriage. He takes it into His heart and treasures it. However, He is very sad if we treat each other badly.

Saint Stephen said, "Remember, each time you feel like arguing or saying something bad to your wife or treating her badly, remember God is watching you. You are not only hurting your wife, but you are hurting God and you are damaging the most holy sacrament of marriage." He said each time you feel like arguing or bad times in marriage that you should remember to turn to God and ask for His help to overcome these differences. He said that if we keep the love of God to the front in our marriages, when we have these difficult moments which everyone gets, when these arguments start, when we feel uneasy with each other, angry with each other, if we just see the love of God and keep it in the front of our marriage, these things will fade away.

I thank Saint Stephen for the help he gave me because our marriage has now become a true marriage of love. Both my wife and I try to think of God in every moment of our marriage.

My wife and I used to argue quite a lot, just about every day but all of a sudden, I started to think about the love of God and how He was looking upon our marriage and how we are one in His eyes, after taking the vow of marriage. All of a sudden, we wouldn't argue so much because every time I felt angry, I just thought about God looking upon our marriage and seeing the love, but also seeing the anger, sometimes the hate, the arguments and sometimes the terrible things we would say to each other, and wondering how God would feel about that. How we were treating the gift that He had given us. How we were spoiling the love that He had given us and that He looks upon each day.

I have come to realize when these things occur in marriage, that they are prompted by the evil one. He puts these thoughts in our mind because he likes to split up marriages, to break marriages, because it is an insult to the Lord. If you can see this every time you feel angry with your partner, every time you just feel so frustrated, and try to remember that your marriage is a gift of God every day, every second, and that He looks upon it and treasures it. When you can see it for what it truly is, then you will find that these little difficulties will just fade away.

I encourage all of you who are married that in every moment of your marriage remember what a sacred gift of God it is. Remember the holy gift your husband or your wife is. Treat them with respect and love and offer that love to God the Father and the Son and the Holy Spirit as a sign of your thanks and love of God.

Divorce

I wondered about all the people who have been divorced, the people who get separated. The Lord said, "You know, this is a terrible thing. Again, this is the evil one who is destroying the sacrament of marriage, making it look worthless. This is what he does with the sacraments, he ridicules them, makes fun of them, makes them look as if they are not worth anything, so that people don't value them, don't treasure them and give them the true esteem they deserve."

The Lord said, "Sometimes marriages do break up. One person may try and keep the marriage together, through love, love of God and love of their partner, but the other one may turn their back on God and their partner. When this happens, when the person is left behind, they shouldn't get married again, they should not become romantically involved with other people again, because then they can be drawn into sin. Instead they should show their love of God every day by maintaining the vow that they made before God and still be acting as if they are married to that person, no matter what the other person does. If the other person sins, it should not lead you into sin. When you sin as well, the sin grows and grows and all of a sudden, your friends may accept what you do and you are now drawing them into sin, and so the sin spreads. This is how evil works."

All of a sudden, my eyes were being opened to all these terrible things that were happening, and I started to treasure marriage more and more. Each day now, our marriage is a joy where before, there used to be so many arguments. If you keep the love of God to the front of your marriage, then you will find that it becomes good. Yes, there will be difficult moments, but turn to the Lord and ask for His help, and He will help you, because He only loves you and only wants to help you.

Saint Matthew and Saint Andrew are so special. They started to teach me all the things I should have learnt in school as a child. I used to be the one in the back of the class, throwing papers around, ignoring the teachers, getting thrown out of the class and learning nothing about God. Now the two of the apostles started to teach me and it was so special. I loved every moment with them.

Jesus

One day, Our Blessed Mother said to me: "My son is coming to you!" and there with me was Jesus, the first time that I had really seen Him, and it was wonderful. He was telling me He loved me, He cared for me and He wanted to forgive me.

I said, "Why me, I've been so bad, and I've committed so many sins?" as I said before, I had almost killed two or three people, and there is Jesus telling me He loved me. I asked, "Why are you appearing to me? Why not a priest, a nun, a holy person…not someone like me!"

He replied, "I love you. I love you the same as everyone else and if I can change someone like you, it shows God's love is for everyone, not for 10% of people, not for a select few."

He said He loves everyone on this earth, regardless of who they are or what they've done, even the worst sinner in the world who has committed the most terrible sins, God loves, and in His mercy wants to forgive, wants to guide them back into His love.

It was the greatest day in my life, Jesus telling me He loved me and He wanted to forgive me. It also was the most difficult because He took me through many of the sins I committed and there was so many of them, it seemed I was sinning every second of my life. He showed me His passion on the cross. He showed me how my sins in some way contributed to His suffering.

Now even the smallest sin, even the thoughts I had about other people, thoughts about disliking them, hating other people, thoughts of anger, frustration with other people seemed so big. They seemed such a weight and if you can imagine those little sins, how big they seemed, imagine how big the big ones were. It was terrible.

Jesus showed me how my sins hurt other people, how often it led them into sin, because maybe they responded in hate, in anger, in violence. Maybe they tried to imitate me because they thought what I was doing was good. He showed me the state of my soul which was putrid, it really was. I felt so embarrassed, so ashamed, I didn't want to be there, but I just couldn't get away and Jesus wouldn't leave me. He was there telling me He loved me. I felt so unworthy.

I saw Jesus in the Garden of Gethsemane taking the pain, the hurt, the suffering from my sins and everyone else's sins from the beginning of time till the end of time onto His heart - no wonder He sweated blood!

I saw the scourging as my sins, the crown of thorns as my sins, I saw Jesus carrying the cross and me sitting on top of it with my pride making it heavier and heavier. I saw each of the nails as my sins and the spear going into His side.

It broke my heart and I was begging Jesus to let me die and send me to hell because I didn't deserve to live anymore. I couldn't stop crying, and yet Jesus was calling out from the cross that He loved me and He wanted to forgive me but I just couldn't believe it because now all that I could see was that in every moment of my life I was hurting Jesus.

Now I saw every time I told a lie I was hurting Jesus as He suffered and died on the cross. Any time I hurt someone else, I was hurting Jesus as He suffered and died on the cross. Any time I was gossiping with others, I was below the cross, gossiping about Jesus as He suffered and died. Any time I made fun of others, I was making fun of Jesus as He suffered and died. Everything I did wrong, I was doing wrong to Jesus as He suffered and died on the cross.

I kept begging Jesus, "Let me die, let me die, I don't want to live." I fell to my knees and I begged Jesus to let me die and to send me to hell because I didn't deserve to live anymore. I just didn't deserve to exist. I didn't <u>want</u> to exist anymore because it was so painful seeing how much Jesus loved me, how sweet He was and how badly I treated Him through my life. I felt so offensive to Him and it hurt me being there. It was the deepest pain I had ever felt in my life, seeing how I had hurt Our Divine Lord. Jesus with the blood running down His face through the suffering kept calling out, "I love you and I want to forgive you."

Truly, it broke my heart. I was sobbing and sobbing like a baby. I was curled up on the floor for 5 hours just crying and crying and begging Jesus to let me die. He kept telling me He loved me and He wanted to forgive me.

After 5 hours I built up the courage and asked Jesus for His forgiveness, and He forgave me. It was incredible, just like a weight being taken from me. It truly was, it was the weight of sin being lifted from me, and it was wonderful! I felt refreshed, I felt renewed, I felt a different person. I knew at that moment that I loved Jesus and that I never wanted to stop loving Him. I knew that His love was the greatest thing to possess in life and I never wanted to lose that again.

I couldn't stop telling Jesus that I loved Him and I wanted to love Him forever. I fell in love with Jesus that day, I really did. I love Jesus and I promised Him at that moment that whatever He asked me, I would do, regardless. No matter what He asked, I would do it and He keeps me to that. Every time I don't want to do something, He reminds me of that promise.

One of the hard things I had to do was to forgive myself. It took me some months to do that, I felt so guilty. I just couldn't let go of it because I remembered all the sins and I kept feeling so guilty that I did those terrible sins. Jesus kept saying, "I have forgiven you, forgive yourself."

Confession

Then Jesus said to me, "Go to confession."

I said, "Wait a minute! Why do I need to go to confession, I've been through all of this! Five hours of crying my eyes out, begging you to let me die and send me to hell. You just took me through all these sins I committed and it was terrible and so painful, and then You said You forgave me. Now why do I need to go to confession?"

I thought Confession was like a power-trip for the priest where you go to confession and you tell him what you've done wrong. Then he tells you off, he gives you some prayers as a punishment, you go outside, you say them as quick as you can and then rush off out of the church. The next time you see the priest you avoid him because he knows how bad you are so you just sort of keep away from him.

The Lord said it's not that at all. "You need to have the grace through the sacrament of Confession to help you through your weaknesses. Confession comes under so much attack because of this grace and other graces received in it." Confession is there to help us, to strengthen us, to purify us, to cleanse us, to heal us, and bring us closer and closer to God. So no wonder the evil one attacks it and makes it look worthless, makes it look as if we don't need it.

He said the holy sacrament of Confession is where the Holy Spirit will cleanse and heal your very soul. That it's important that you go and that you confess all your sins.

So off I went to confession and I went into the confessional box and I said, "Please Father, forgive me, for I have sinned. I stole this little thing and told this little lie, and forgive me for anything else I have done," and that covered all the big sins, all the terrible ones, because I didn't want to confess them, I didn't want the priest to know how bad I really was.

When I came out of the confessional box, the Lord said to me, "Don't do that!" He said: "Understand, when you don't confess all your sins that you hold on to pain and hurt and suffering." He said, "If you do not confess all of your sins it is easy for satan to lead you into more and more sin because so often you feel bad about yourself but also you have that sin residing on your heart, on your very soul, and it's a weakness there, it's a doorway where evil can enter and lead you into more and more sin and lead you further away from God."

The Lord said, "Understand also that I've been with you from your first breath and I will be with you till your last breath. I know everything you have done. I know every sin you've committed, every bad thought you've had, every bad feeling, every bad word, everything you've done! Even when you've been alone in sinning, and you thought no one was there, I was there watching you. There is nothing you can hide from Me and when you try to, you are only hurting yourself. Understand, I know you inside out but I love you so much, I will forgive you anything.

"I gave My life for your forgiveness, I shed My blood to cleanse your very soul, and all I ask is that you come to confession; you recognize your sins, you confess them all, hold nothing back, understanding I know them already. I love you so much I'll forgive you anything, anything at all, but please don't hold it back, because when you do, all you're doing is hurting yourself."

He said, "Don't be embarrassed in front of the priest because it is the Holy Spirit that is acting through the priest and the priest won't hold on to those sins. The Holy Spirit will help him to let go of them, and so when he sees you, they are not on his mind. Often, they are just gone. Understand where these feelings of shame, of embarrassment come from. It is satan working on your pride so that you won't confess."

What Jesus showed me was that it is the Holy Spirit in the confessional box that touches your soul, your very spirit and lifts the stain of sin from you. He said, "I want you to look at your own sins and see them, come to terms with them and then come to Me and say "Lord, forgive me,' and I will, because I love you. I will forgive you anything."

Prayers of Penance

I went back to Confession the next day and I confessed all the big sins I could remember. I was in there, crying and I felt so sorry for the priest, I was in there such a long time. Then I came out of the confessional box, and I said the penance the priest gave me very quickly, almost like a steam train, and then rushed off out of the church.

The Lord said to me, "Don't do that!" He said, "That penance is not a punishment and is not just a prayer you should just say and forget about. The penance is a guidance from the Holy Spirit to help you overcome your weaknesses, to help you overcome your sins and you should take the time and look at those prayers and ask the Holy Spirit to show you the message that He's giving to you in the prayers of penance. If you do that, you'll see a line that stands out and that's the message from the Holy Spirit for you, to help you."

Our Father

So, I started to do that, and I saw in the Our Father the words **"Our Father"**.

The Lord was reminding me that He was everyone's father, not just mine! With all the wonderful things that were happening in my life now, I was starting to think I was someone special to God, I was above others but the Lord was reminding me that He loves us all the same, that He's the Father of everyone. How sad it is today that many people don't believe that!

So often, they look up to others who may be having experiences like me, who may be having visions, who may be a stigmatist, who may be gifted in special ways. They look up to them and think, "God must love them more than He loves me!" However, that's not true, God loves us <u>all</u> the same. There's no difference in His love for us. The only difference is how much we love Him and we should never forget that and we should never look up to others in that way.

We should only look up to God, worship and adore God and thank God for the gifts that He expresses through many different people, never seeing others as above us. Always see that we are all equal in God's eyes regardless of what gifts He gives.

I saw: **Our daily bread**. Give us our daily bread.

The Lord was calling me to daily Eucharist and now I started to see that it was essential that if I wanted to live close to God, I had to have daily Eucharist that if I loved God, surely I would want Him filling me every day! If I love the Father, Jesus and the Holy Spirit, surely I will want union with Jesus and through Jesus with the Holy Trinity every day. The only way that's possible is through the Eucharist, through the Bread of Life, the Wine of Forgiveness.

I found the more I went to the Eucharist, the more I had this desire to go again and again, as when I didn't receive the Lord, there'd be an emptiness within me. Daily Eucharist had become essential, and all of a sudden I saw that it was the Eucharist that was strengthening me, giving me the power to overcome my weaknesses, that there is this God-given power to see where I was going wrong in life and to help me step past that by the grace of the Holy Spirit.

I saw that without the Eucharist it is so easy for me to be drawn away from God because without the Eucharist, I am relying on myself, but living in the Eucharist, I am relying on Jesus and the power of His Holy Spirit. So I discovered that the Eucharist is essential for life, essential to living.

The Lord said, "Unless you eat of My body and drink of My blood you shall not have life within you." It is so true. Without the Eucharist, we're dead because we're living in this dead world, this world full of sin and full of self, full of suffering, full of pain. When we live in the Eucharist, we live in the joy, the love, the happiness, the strength of our divine Lord.

So for me and for every Catholic, the Eucharist is essential! It is the centre of our faith, it is the core of our faith, and if you call yourself Catholic you must be living a Eucharistic life otherwise you are Catholic in name only. If you call yourself Catholic, you must believe in God in the Eucharist, you must believe in Jesus in the Eucharist; He's told us in Scripture and He shows us in every Mass and all we need to do is open our heart, open our very soul to see that truth in the Eucharist, to see God in the Eucharist.

Catholics must live the Eucharistic faith because that is our faith. Without the Eucharist, we have a hollow, an empty faith. Without the Eucharist, truly we are dead to God and full of ourselves. The Eucharistic way is the way of Christ, is the Catholic way, and is the way to live.

I saw, **Thy kingdom come**.

Again I saw that when I receive the Eucharist, the kingdom of God was coming into my heart and filling me. When I took Jesus in the Eucharist with me to everyone that I met, then His kingdom would reach out through me and touch them and bring them to His kingdom. All I had to do was say Yes! in every Eucharist to Jesus to doing His will, to taking Him to the world and letting His light shine from my soul so that others could be brought to that glorious kingdom of love which is the Father, Son and Holy Spirit.

I saw, **To forgive others** because I saw that if God forgave me, surely if I want to be Christ-like, I must forgive others. Jesus forgave those who killed Him, who abused Him; He forgave them all. He offered forgiveness to each one and surely if I want to be Christ-like, I must be the same, that anyone who abused me, said bad things about me, treated me badly, that I must be forgiving them automatically, holding no resentment, no anger.

As the moment I felt hatred, anger or resentment towards anyone, then I was holding on to evil in my heart and I was stepping away from God. With forgiveness, it helped me grow in God because it pushed away these bad thoughts, those bad feelings and took evil away from me allowing God's goodness to fill me.

I discovered that forgiveness is an essential part of being Christian, of being Christ-like, of being Catholic. What a shame it is that many Catholics today hold on to anger, to resentment, to hatred. How the evil one laughs because you hold on to what he wants you to hold on to and you don't let go of what God wants you to let go of.

I saw, **Lead us not into temptation**. The Lord was saying to me: Don't go to bars, don't go to night clubs, don't go to pubs, keep yourself away from temptation.

I saw the words: **Deliver us from evil**.

With so many difficult times in my life, often I thought I could overcome them myself. Satan began to attack me physically and in the beginning I thought I could overcome him but what I had forgotten is he is a fallen archangel, he is very powerful. I am human, I am weak, I cannot overcome him! In myself I am bound to fail. But in "deliver us from evil" the Lord was saying when I turn to Him I can overcome evil because Jesus has already defeated satan and if I give myself completely to Jesus in every Eucharist there is nothing that satan can do to me. In the Eucharist, when I fill myself with Jesus, I am filled with the power of Heaven, the power of God and it is satan who is afraid of me.

The Lord was saying to me, "You can only overcome evil in your life by the power God, in the name of the Father and the name of Jesus and the name of the Holy Spirit. There is no other way." You must turn to God in humility and accept that and then you will overcome evil but when you turn to yourself, you are bound to fail.

God also showed me that if I turn to Jesus on the cross, I <u>would</u> be delivered from evil because Jesus on the cross had defeated evil. So if I embrace His cross, I have nothing to fear in life. I should be concerned about nothing because in Jesus, I become the victor. In Him, I've won.

Today many Catholics are afraid. They walk around as if they are the defeated, forgetting that we are the victors in Christ. So many Catholics are afraid of the end-times coming, of an anti-Christ coming and they don't understand that if we cling to the cross of Christ, then we have won, and it is satan that fears us. If we carry that cross with us wherever we go, fearing nothing, then the victory is ours!

Yet so many walk around afraid. Our faith is not one of fear, it is one of trust in God's victory, and we must carry that victory with us everywhere, carry that cross on our soul, open our arms and embrace Jesus on the cross and say, "I live in Your victory and I am taking Your victory with me wherever I go."

When you confront evil, do not fear it, do not be afraid, because truly it's evil that fears us!

People should understand that if you live your Eucharistic faith, that the least one of us, the weakest, the most fragile one of us living in the Eucharist is more powerful than satan himself. This is because we have the power of God with us, the power of Heaven, it is satan who fears us. It is only our fears, our weaknesses, our doubts, our disbelief that changes that!

If we can have that total commitment to God, that total commitment to our Eucharistic Lord, holding tightly on to His cross, carrying that cross with us wherever we go, then the victory of Christ will shine so brightly in this world that pain and suffering will flee, darkness will go, and the victory of God will rule supreme in this world and paradise will be here with us!

However, it begins with every Catholic believing in that, living in that way, and not being afraid. Being like those early martyrs, being like the early Church, trusting unto death and not fearing death itself but seeing death as the gift it is - the gift that can lead to Heaven where our Lord will be waiting with His arms open wide to embrace you in love.

Fear of dying

There are many Catholics who are afraid of dying but why should we be? It is a natural part of life. It is through death we can come to eternal love with God, eternal life with God, so why fear it? When you have a fear of death, you are allowing satan, you are allowing evil to work on you, because in fear, all of a sudden you start to doubt, all of a sudden you start to lose your trust in God. If you do not fear death, if you do not fear anything, then that trust is strong, that faith is strong, and truly you can live the Catholic life. The life that Jesus calls each one of us to. Fear is not part of our faith. Trust, belief and love are.

Also, when you are trying to bring people to God, if you try and bring them by fear, you know what happens? Once they overcome their fear, often they go away again but if you bring them to God by love, they always stay. Love and trust are keys to our faith.

Hail Mary

I saw in the Hail Mary's when I was given those as a penance, 'Holy Mary', and the Lord was saying to me that if I wanted to be holy, that I should imitate Mary. I should see how obedient she was to God's will and that I should try and be that obedient, too.

Today that means to be obedient to the Catholic Church because it is the House of the Father, it is the Body of Christ and it is filled with the Holy Spirit.

So when we are obedient to the Church it is being obedient to God. That obedience can be like a protective blanket around you because it protects you from all error, from all heresy. When you look to the Catholic truth, you look to the truth of God, and when you live to that truth, it keeps you away from being led down the wrong path.

Today, sadly, so many Catholics are reading many things that are not Catholic and listening to things that are not Catholic and absorbing some of that. I wonder why they do it, because we have everything in Catholicism, why do we need to look elsewhere? All we need to do is be obedient to our faith and then we are living in the completeness of God's truth.

Marriage

Today so many Catholics are disobedient, and they wonder why they have problems in their lives. So many get divorced and yet Jesus was very clear about that. We shouldn't get divorced. So many do it because they have a problem getting on with their husband or wife and the arguments gets so bad, life gets so difficult.

Marriage is a sacred vow before God and we should never forget that - it's a sacrament. A sacrament that should not be damaged, destroyed or broken. Sometimes of course people for various reasons cannot live together. Well, if that's the case, you still have to hold on to your sacramental promise.

If you have to live apart, you cannot get married again, or you cannot find another partner, because the moment you do, you become adulterous, and you start to sin and you start to become disobedient to God. Marriage is for life, marriage is eternal, it is a promise you have made to God and a promise which should not be broken.

The only time a marriage can be dissolved is when the church gives an annulment for valid reasons because then God in His merciful love, is correcting what should never have happened.

Abortion - Contraception

Today, many Catholics are having abortions but abortion is murder, is killing an innocent child, and it does not matter what the world says. Some in the world say it is not a baby yet it is a nothing but from the moment of conception there is life there, God-given life, and the moment you destroy that life, you are offending God.

So many Catholics are using contraception and many say, Well, everybody else in the world is doing it and it makes life easier, that the Church does not know what it is talking about.

All people are doing are making excuses for being disobedient, and <u>how</u> satan laughs! Contraception <u>is</u> wrong because it interferes with the processes of life that God has created. So now these people are standing against God and opposing God and actually becoming anti-Christ in their ways.

Contraception is wrong, and it should not be used, no matter what the reason. For women taking the oral contraceptive, there are medical studies that are showing it is very bad for you.

In 1995 the World Health Organization reported that women taking particular brands of contraceptive were at risk of thrombo-embolism. The results were:

Non users - five to ten per hundred thousand.

Pills containing levonorgestrel/norethisterone - fifteen to forty per one hundred thousand.

Pills containing Desogstrel/gestodene - thirty to eighty per one hundred thousand.

Even those who may use the pill for as little as one to six months are at risk of developing cancer of the cervix (190%) as compared with non users.

(Ref: Wilks.J. B.Pharm. M.P.S. '*A Consumer's Guide to the Pill and Other Drugs*' Freedom Pub., Vic.1996 p.34)

Until 1999 Japan rejected the legislation of oral contraceptives for health reasons. The probability of a women developing breast cancer in Japan is one in fifty. In America it is one in eight. In Australia it is one in sixteen. (Ref: Ibid).

The 'Daily Telegraph' in Sydney, Australia on January 25th 1999 reported, "Six young New Zealand women have died from blood clots after taking popular brands of contraception, aged between nineteen and thirty two."

There are other studies like this that often are hidden away, you do not hear about them.

You should be aware that what you are taking is not good for you! It alters the processes that God has created in your body, it fights against the natural processes of your body and there must be a price to pay. Sometimes when people stop taking the oral contraceptives and try and have children they find they cannot have them. So many become this way because they have been taking the oral contraceptive and now they seek children and they wonder why they cannot have them.

You should not be taking these things. You should understand also that within the Catholic Church there is a method called the 'Billings Method' which is ninety eight to ninety nine percent effective in family planning.

You should speak to the Church about this. It is approved of by the Church, it does not interfere with the processes that God has created, and that is what you should be using...natural family planning. Speak to the Church, talk to them, do not listen to the world, listen to God's Church.

If you are using contraception, what you are doing is wrong, and you must stop, because as you live in this error, as you live in this wrong, you are not living your faith and you are opening yourself more and more to evil.

There is so much that we accept in disobedience, and then we wonder why we suffer in our lives - so much suffering in our families, so much suffering in the world, and it all comes from disobedience. If we have an obedient faith, we will find happiness, we will find joy, we will find peace, we will find love, we will find security!

That is what God has offered us from the beginning! However, from when Adam first sinned, from that first moment of disobedience, we have been stepping away from God's offer of goodness, and we have continued to do so throughout the history of mankind, and today we do so over and over. We make so many excuses to make disobedience acceptable. We say, "Everyone else is doing it – it is okay. The Church does not know what it's talking about. "

In truth it is the Church that knows what it is talking about because it has the wisdom of God, and we should live to that wisdom. Not doing so, makes us very foolish.

I saw, Holy Mary, **full of grace**.

The Lord said to me that if I wanted to be filled with grace, if I wanted to be filled with gifts, again I had to be obedient, because this obedience that Mary had allowed her to be filled with the Holy Spirit.

It will be the same for me and for anyone else, if you want charisms and gifts to grow in your life, if you want to be graced by God in a special way, have that obedient faith and then you open your heart and soul to the Holy Spirit and He will pour in the gifts, He will pour in the graces.

Obedience is the key to our faith. We must start living that way, being an example of obedient love to the world. It is this that will show the world that we are Christ-like, it is this that will show the world that we truly love God and that we truly love our fellow man. It is this that will show the love of God to the world and change the world.

Glory Be.

I saw in the **Glory Be**'s to glorify God in my life.

When I had started praying for people for healing and there were many wonderful healings starting to happen such as blind people seeing, cripples walking and deaf people hearing, all of a sudden I started to think how special I was, how good I was. However, God was reminding me it's the Father, the Son and the Holy Spirit who do everything, all I do is pray for healing like any person can do.

If you believe in God, if you persevere, if you trust in His healing power, God will work through any of you as He works through me, because He loves us all the same. What He will do through me He will do through others because God wants to use each one of us who are part of His Church. He wants to use each one of us to pour out His love to change the world, to make the world a holy, a happy place and so He will use us as instruments for that. So all you have to do is believe, persevere and trust in God, and He will use you.

Those prayers of penance mean so much to me now because as I look, I see God giving me lots of guidance.

Healing in Confession

Confession is such a wonderful sacrament, a very powerful healing sacrament.

Often people wonder why they are not healed. They go to doctors and many other places, yet do not get healed and the problems continue in their lives, physical, emotional, spiritual problems, and people wonder why there is no healing happening. These people maybe go for prayers and they do not get healed and still they wonder why they are not being healed. So often it is because they are holding on to sin. When you hold on to sin, you hold on to the pain, the hurt, the suffering that comes with it - how can you expect to be healed?

Confession is a powerful healing sacrament. When you go to confession, confess all the sins, all those ones you have hidden away, all those ones you are ashamed of, embarrassed of, you can't tell the priest about; confess all your sins.

Then through the priest, let the Holy Spirit pour out His healing love, His healing power to cleanse and heal your very soul. Doing that, you will find for many that is where the healing begins in life. If you hold on to sin, if you hold on to pain, to hurt, to suffering, how can you expect to be healed?

Many people say, "Well, we don't need to go to confession, we go directly to God." What Jesus said in Scripture to the apostles was, "Whose sins you forgive, they are forgiven." Here is God giving His power to men, in a very clear direction. He said to Peter: "What you bind on earth, is bound in Heaven," thereby giving Peter authority.

So if Peter or succeeding Popes who that authority has been passed on to, said, that priests by the grace of God can forgive sins and that people need to come to Confession for forgiveness, for their soul to be healed, their heart to be healed, their life to be healed, then that is bound in Heaven!

It does not matter whether you believe that or not, that is the truth of Heaven and if you do not believe that, when you face Jesus on the Final Day, He is going to ask you why, and I wonder what you are going to say?

This is a deception of evil to keep people away from Confession to say you can go directly to God.

People sometimes say, "In the Our Father we ask God for forgiveness." Yes, we do. What God is saying to us in the Our Father is that we have to come to God for forgiveness but when Jesus said to the apostles, "Whose sins you forgive," He said that we have to come through the priests, we have to come through the men that God has given power to.

When the Popes have confirmed this is the truth then that is bound in Heaven. You must believe that because if you do not you are being anti-Christ, you are going against what Jesus Our Lord has said, you are opposing Christ Himself and you are becoming anti-Christ in the world.

What happens with frequent confession is you keep seeing the little errors, the little wrongs, and the big ones that you are doing, it makes you aware of them. It keeps you aware of them and as you keep seeing them, as you keep looking at them, then you try to overcome them by the grace of God, and He gives you that grace. If you don't look at them, it is so easy for them to get bigger and bigger. Then you can get led into more and more sin, worse and worse sin, because now you are being blinded to the wrongs in your life. Confession opens your eyes to where you are going wrong, and it opens your heart to the grace and strength of God to overcome your wrongs.

So now in Confession and in the prayers in penance, I was

seeing so much. Often I would see the same lines over and over and I thought, Why is this happening? I got that yesterday and the day before and last week. The Lord explained, "You have not overcome this sin yet and I keep giving you the same message until you do, and then eventually, I will give you another one."

That is how it works, just like a building process. You get over one sin, then He helps you over the next one and over the next one.

The Lord said, "The important thing is that you recognize your mistakes and once you recognize them, come to Confession and ask for forgiveness. Do not push them to the side and say they are not important. Understand that it is important to get rid of every sin."

Confession as an Eye-opener

The Lord explained that in Confession there are many gifts and many graces for mankind. If you open your heart and accept the Holy Spirit within in the sacrament, what He will do is open your eyes to the sin in the world. He will take away the blindness that many of us have, that I have all the time. I used to think I was better than other people. I used to see people starving in other countries, and I would give five dollars to satisfy my conscience. The Lord was asking, "Why are you giving that money? You are not giving it because you want to help them. You are just doing it to make yourself feel a bit more comfortable. If you truly want to help these people, you will reach out in love and give as much as you can and you will try and help as much as you can, because they are God's children, too and I love them the same as I love you." He continued, "Understand, when you are wasting in your life, when you are leading a comfortable life, you are doing it at the expense of others. They are starving because you are wasting. Look at these people and see the price they are paying for your luxurious life. Reach out to them in love and help them as much as you can."

He said, "See how satan blinds you to this. How you can even think at times that your life is not so good even though you have got many of the luxuries. There are people starving, eating from rubbish tips. How can you allow this to happen if you are truly a Christian? Surely you can only reach out in love to these people and help."I used to turn away from drunks and drug addicts and beggars on the street and never give them much. The Lord said to me, "Why are you doing that? When you are doing that, you are turning away from Me and this is satan again leading you away from Me. In each person, see Me. Even in the people in the gutter, see Me and reach out and love them. When you turn away from these people, because you think that if I give them money, they might spend it on alcohol, they might spend it on drugs, they might waste it, - when you are turning away from people in this way, you are putting conditions on your love. Love should be unconditional. When you see people in need, you should reach out and want to help them because at that moment, if you turn away, that might be the moment they are lost. However, in that moment, if you turn to them, and help them, that might be the moment they are saved." Of course we have to make sure the help we give does not let people continue to sin but we must help in a good way. What a responsibility we have and so I try and help everyone. Sometimes I forget.

The Lord said, "It is so important that you share because that is part of being a Christian, a Catholic." Today, so many people can be blinded to that and only see their own needs. It is important to see the needs of others.

All of a sudden, Confession became so special because it started to show me many things in my life where I was going wrong. The Lord advised, "That is what the sacrament is for. It is to put you right in your life. It is a sacrament that brings you a step closer to God every time you receive it with an open heart and the more you receive the sacrament of confession, the closer to God you will come."

How often to go to Confession

In the beginning, I had started going to Mass once a week and Confession once a month, and I thought I was really saintly, because before that, I used to go only at Easter to keep the faith. Our Blessed Mother suggested to me, and also Jesus later on, to go to Confession more. I thought once a month was a lot but then I started going once a week and now several times a week. Our Blessed Mother explained to me that Confession is a special sacrament that is often underrated. So many people ignore it or reject it or will not go to it. Of course, this comes from the evil one again, trying to stop us receiving the benefit of the gift from God through His sacrament of confession.

Just increase the sacrament and you will find many gifts for you that the Holy Spirit, Jesus and the Father are longing to give you through the wonderful sacrament of Confession that is so forgotten today. It is forgotten because satan works on our pride to say to us, "We don't

82

need to go to confession. We haven't sinned. We haven't done too much wrong." Understand when you feel this way, that is when you probably need to go to Confession most of all. So please, increase confession.

Confession is also a strengthening for the priest because each time the priest hears confession, the Holy Spirit is flowing through him and strengthens the priest. So, the priest is benefitting from your Confession also.

Confession is an essential part of our faith, and you <u>must</u> go. If you are not going, start going maybe once a year. If you are going once a year, maybe go once a month. If you are going once a month, maybe go twice a month. If you are going twice a month, go once a week. Just increase the sacrament, and you will find, as I have, that it will change your life. It will bring so much peace into you, it will bring a strength into your life.

Confession is more than forgiveness, it is more than healing, it is more than receiving graces and gifts. It is full of wonders, it is full of joys, a true treasure from God, and we should not ignore it.

Gifts of the Spirit

For those who are charismatic, and you want your gifts to grow, confession is essential because if you hold on to sin, then you have little barriers on your soul to the Holy Spirit filling you. So the more you go to confession the more you get rid of these little barriers and the more the Holy Spirit can fill you with His graces and with His gifts.

So, as a charismatic, I find going to confession frequently also opens me up to the power of the Holy Spirit more, and it will be the same for each one of you. Of course every Christian by their baptism is charismatic, it's whether you accept or deny the charisms in your life.

The same Sins over and over

I would go out of the confessional box after I confessed my sins and I seemed to be doing the same things over and over. I thought, "How can I do that? You know, Jesus is talking to me, Our Blessed Mother, and yet I am doing the same sins over and over." The Lord said, "You are human. You will do these things, you will make mistakes, that is part of being human. If you did not make mistakes, if you did not sin, if you were perfect, you would be in Heaven."

Often I would hold on to the guilt of it and Jesus said, "It is satan who keeps putting these thoughts in your mind so that you will not let go of these sins, even after I have forgiven you. Realize, when you have confessed truly from your heart, and you have tried your hardest not to sin again, you are forgiven. Let go of the guilt. Remember the sins so that you do not do them again but let go of the guilt." It is when we do not we are denying Jesus' sacrifice on the cross, because from the cross, He is offering us all forgiveness. He is offering it to us, and we go and ask for it, and then we refuse it.

The Lord explained that so many people hold on to the guilt of their sin. They have been forgiven in the confessional box, but they hold on to the guilt of their sin, they just cannot let go because they feel unworthy. They think, "How can God forgive me?"

Of course, if you keep hold of that, often it makes you

nervous, unwell. Often it leads you into more sin. I met a woman in Perth who, for over twenty years, had held on to something that she had been forgiven. Now she was not a healthy woman, but the Lord lifted that from her within a few seconds once she let go of her sins that had been forgiven, it was like a weight being taken from her.

Over and over the Lord says to me, "Keep looking forward, do not look back. Look forward now at how good you can be. Look forward in My love. Look forward to living as I want you to live. Live in love, share this love with others. Do your best to atone for what you have done wrong in the past but do not keep looking back and thinking how bad you were and what a bad person you were."

Live in Love

Jesus explained to me, "Love is the most important thing in your life. You should build your life on love because God is love. If you build your life on love, you do not feel angry with anyone, you do not get upset with anyone, you do not want to hurt anyone, you do not want to have more than others, you want to share with others so they can live as you do, so they can be as happy as you are. You want to bring God's love to everyone so that they understand the Father, Jesus, and the Holy Spirit as you do. When you truly live in love, in God's love, the true love, you will live completely in Him, and everything you do you do for Him. Every word you speak is a word of love, God's love. Every action is an action of God's love. Every breath is a breath of God's love. Everything you do you do for God. When you look upon your neighbours, when you look upon each other, you only see God's love in them, and it will be difficult to get angry. You will see past that. You will see the love within them and reach out in God's love to touch their love to help it grow, so they too can grow and become a flower in God's love, a rose in God's love like Saint Theresa." To live in God's love is very hard for most of us because at times we feel so frustrated with people, so angry with people, at times we feel we deserve more than others, at times we can be a bit greedy, a bit selfish. All these thoughts take us away from God's love, because in God's love you only want to share, you only want everyone to have what you have, that treasure of God's love within but how many of us truly feel that way?

When others hurt you

Our Blessed Mother encouraged me to be like Jesus in all I did. She said to be Christian, to be Catholic, which is the completeness of Christianity, means I must live the way of Jesus and try to be like Jesus in all that I do. One of the things she explained to me was that in the Heart of Jesus is forgiveness and love for all people without conditions. He loves everyone and He wants to forgive everyone, and if I wanted to be Christian, Christ-like, that I had to be the same.

I used to find that very hard because I was angry with many people but now I realized the moment I felt bad towards anyone, first of all I was feeling bad towards a creation of God's love, a creation that was created through and in Jesus Christ Our Lord. So surely I must be hurting God doing so. So now, all of a sudden, I wanted to love everyone and forgive everyone.

Even today, so many people at times do things that maybe hurt me a little. Now Jesus tells me to thank Him for the opportunity that arises in each of these moments so I can show true love in my forgiveness of others. The more I do this, the more natural this seems to be and the more peace I feel within myself. Before, when I had anger and hate and unforgiveness, I felt so bitter, so unsettled within. Now by the grace of God I can forgive and let go of anything, there is always peace in my heart and it should be the same for each one of you.

If you want to be Catholic, if you want to be Christian, if you want to be Christ-like, then in your heart there must be an automatic forgiveness and an automatic love for every person. Unfortunately, so many of us hold on to anger, to resentment. So many of us seek revenge but that is not the way of Christ. Many people today are afraid of an anti-Christ but people should understand that when you live this unforgiving way, that the anti-Christ is in you because you are living against the will of Jesus. Jesus' will is that you forgive and you love everyone regardless of what they do to you. You must love and forgive unto death because that is what Jesus did and when we want to be Christ-like, we must do the same.

Longing for Jesus' love

Jesus' love is so special. Everything is there for us in Jesus' love. Before, I did not recognize that, but when the Lord touched me, I began to understand what love truly is and how much God loves us and how we are turning our backs on Him through the pride within us, the pride that satan stirs up all the time. He is there all the time trying to turn us away from God because our souls are so special, so much of a treasure. Satan just wants to take them from God. Yet Jesus said, "If you live in My love, he cannot harm you, he cannot do anything to you. Accept My love within you and live in My love."

I asked, "How can I do that?" He answered, "The sacraments, I fill you with My love in the sacraments. They are there to help you and strengthen you. When you receive Communion and receive My love within, I fill your soul, your spirit, your very being, if you will accept and believe and allow Me to, because I give you the free choice to accept or deny My love within. When you receive the sacraments, understand they are not just for yourself. When My love touches you within, it is not just for yourself. You have to share it amongst others and when you give to others, you receive more from Me, because the more you give, the more you receive."

The Lord said, "When you receive My love in the sacraments, go out and share it with people, share My love in everything you do. When you do that, you are spreading My love and it touches others. No matter how far away they are from Me, if you show love to them, it may not affect them straight away, but maybe a few months, a few years down the track, they remember how you acted in love, how you acted in God's love, and it brings so many back. This is how the Church grows."

The Lord said, "Many people come to church and love God. They come to Mass often, receive the sacraments often and see this as a personal thing between them and God." Well, that is partly true. It is a personal thing between us and God, but God said, "I ask you to go out and share Me with everyone." Jesus asks us to share His love and to love everyone as He loved everyone and in that way help the Church grow.

I have heard so many people say that there are not many vocations. Not many people are coming to Mass. The numbers are dropping. Why is this happening? Why is God allowing it? It is happening because we as Jesus' followers are not doing what He asked of us, which is to share His love, to spread His love, to take His love to others. Not standing up in the street corner and waving placards around and saying, "The end of the world is near, repent!" Not that, not being condemning or judgmental, but being kind, loving, generous. Sharing your love with others, helping those in need, being a friend to all, because that is what Jesus is to us and that is what He expects us to be to others. This is how the Church will grow, through love and through kindness.

The Lord said, "If My followers do not do this, who is going to do it, who can I ask if I can't ask those who love Me? Those who so often feel ashamed, embarrassed to talk about Me." Again this is the evil one who puts that within you. He builds up your pride, you don't want to be hurt, embarrassed or made fun of. You just feel you cannot speak about Jesus. Often when you are standing amongst a group of friends you can talk about anything, anything except Jesus. I was like that, afraid to speak. The Lord said, "Speak about Me. Speak about Me in your actions, the way you act with people, the way you love them. When you are doing this, tell them when you are being this way it is because you love Jesus and you want to share His love with them."

Sharing about Jesus

The Lord showed me one day how this works. I was in the restroom at work, and a man walked in called Mark. The Lord said, "Speak to him!" I thought, "Oh no, not in here surely!' He said, "Yes, speak to him." So I did. We were in there for about an hour which is unusual for men. During the time, Mark said to me, "That is incredible. My wife has just left me and taken my two children, and you seem to know everything I was thinking, you answered every question I had on my mind. I had so many problems. You have answered them all for me. How did you do it?"I built up the courage and said to him, "Jesus speaks to me, Jesus tells me." I thought he would laugh and make fun of me, but he accepted it and he started to think about God. What Jesus showed me there was if you trust in Him, if you step out in faith, He is not going to let you down. He will help you to touch others and bring others to Him. Do you really believe that if we step forward in Jesus that He is going to desert us? He will not. He will be there, helping us and guiding us, helping us to bring others back to Him.

Taking His Light out

When the Lord forgave me, I fell in love with Him, I really did. That day, I found the love of Jesus and it changed my whole life. Every day now I ask the Lord for that love. I almost beg Him because I ache for that love, I just want that love to fill me.

He explained everyone should be this way. Longing for His love to come in their heart to fill them completely so they can live as they should. Now every day as His love touches me, it shows me how wrong we live, even the devout at times allow pride to fill them so that they do not live as God wants them to.

As His love touches me every day and fills me, I see how graceful God is to reach down to me, to touch me with His love. When He does that, I see so much darkness out there and so much darkness within myself. The Lord said, "When you are filled with My love, you are filled with light. Take that light out to everyone." This is what every Christian should do and especially Catholics. When you receive the sacrament of communion, remember you are filled with His love, it is your duty to share that love with others, but so often we do not. So often we think about ourselves and we leave the church and we do not reach out to others to share that joy, that love of God which He has placed inside of us. Not sharing that is selfishness.

As Catholics, we should be out there, sharing that joy, sharing that love that God gives us in the sacraments, especially communion, sharing it so that others can find that treasure, that wonderful treasure of His love that is there for everyone.

The Church God gave Mankind

The Catholic Church is the Church that Jesus Christ Our Lord, God Himself, gave to mankind, that He gave in love. Now there are many other churches, but they are created by man, in frustration, in anger. Jesus asked me one day, "Do you want to belong to the Church I created in love or the church men have created in their frustration?" I answered, "Of course to Your Church of love." He said, "Well then, you must be Catholic because this is the Church I gave to mankind through Peter and the authority

91

and power I gave to Peter resides with each of his successors, nowhere else. The completeness of My truth on earth is Catholicism." That doesn't mean that there are only Catholics in Heaven. There are Muslims, Jews, Hindus, Protestants, all sorts of people as in many of the other faiths the truth of God does reside to some degree but not in the completeness that is in Catholicism. If those people live to the fullness of God that they know, then Heaven too can be theirs. However, it is our duty to spread the full truth of God to the world and not to be ashamed or afraid to do so.

Today, many Catholics are looking for ecumenism, for unity. So often, when we look for unity, we are prepared to give some of our faith away. Maybe not to be so obedient to the Church or its teachings. Not to have such a belief in the sacraments and all of a sudden, when we do that, we no longer become Catholic, but we are Protestant. Now we are changing and *protesting* against what God has given us. Yes, we must look for unity, we must reach out to all people in love, welcome them into our church, because it is the church for everyone. When the Protestants come back to the Catholic Church, they will bring a richness with them. A richness of community, of understanding of Holy Scripture. A richness of Charismatic gifts, and they will make our Church stronger. We must remember to welcome them in the truth that is Catholicism and not to change that truth and we must never be afraid to stand up and proclaim the complete truth of God on earth.

Terrorism

I was in America on September 11 and I was flying at the time when the terrible tragedies happened. I landed ten minutes later at Philadelphia airport. Then I saw the terrible tragedy unfolding, I felt so sad as most people did and my first feelings were ones of forgiveness for those people on the planes who had died and those people in the buildings who had died. I prayed that God would forgive them their sins. I prayed for both the victims and for those who had committed those terrible crimes. I saw those who committed those acts of terrorism had done so because anger and hatred had built up inside them from being treated so badly, or their families or their nations being treated badly. So they had responded in the bad way, influenced by evil. I saw my duty as a Christian was to pray for their forgiveness and to forgive them, because that is what Christ would expect from me.

He said, turn the other cheek, forgive your enemies, love them. This seems to be the hardest commandment for many, to love your enemies, but that is what Jesus calls us to. I say to people: If Jesus was standing in front of you today, and you said to Him, should we bomb Afghanistan (or Iraq), what do you think He would say? He wouldn't say yes, He would say no! He would say, love them, forgive them and help them to stop doing these things. But sadly, many Christians can't accept that.Some say, they killed our friends, our family, our people, surely we have got to respond. But when Jesus came to Israel, to the Holy Land, the Jews at that time were saying the same things about the Romans, they are killing us, they are taking our land, come and lead us against them! But Jesus said, "That is not My way. My way is of peace, of love and of forgiveness."

The reason that we have these problems is, that we have this double standard. When many see young Arabs being killed, houses being bulldozed down, many Christians

 don't think anything about it. There is a deafening silence. How many of us here are standing up saying, this is wrong! This has got to stop! They see the Jews being killed, and the whole world is shouting, this is wrong, which of course it is. We have to treat people equally. We have to treat Jew, Moslem, Christian, the same. We have to respect them all the same. If we don't do that, then we'll pay this price.

I am not pro-Arab, I am not pro-Israeli, I love Jew, Christian, Moslem, the same, as we should, as God calls us to. But it was interesting, recently people were talking about these terrorist attacks the Arabs have done, and, of course, they shouldn't be happening at all, but some forget the terrorist attacks the Jewish people are doing on the Arabs, killing their children, assassinating people. And who is saying this is wrong, this has got to stop? We have to stand up as Christians and be Christ-like and say, "Everyone is equal." When an Arab dies, that is a bad loss to the world, that life is valuable. When a Jew dies, that is a bad loss, that life is valuable, they are equal. When a Christian dies, that life is valuable. Not see Arabs as less than others, because as long as we are going to do that, they are going to hate us.

How sad it was as I travelled around the world in the months following September 11, to see so many Catholics, so many Christians, crying out for revenge. Crying out for an eye for an eye and a tooth for a tooth. That is not the

Christian way. That is the Old Testament way of Judaism. Jesus came to fulfil the Old Testament, it is completed in Him, and as Christians, we live the New Testament, referring to the Old Testament, but we live to what Christ Our Lord said. That means to forgive and to love. Jesus is the fulfilment of the Old Testament. One of the fruits of the crucifixion is the ability to forgive. The New Testament tells us that we must love and forgive everyone – not kill them when we feel it is justified. Realize the difference between revenge and justice. Revenge is not of God, justice is.

How many Catholics live like that? So many I heard crying for blood. Do you think Jesus was crying out for blood? Jesus was crying out that Catholics would stand up and call for forgiveness, love and understanding. However, the vast majority of Catholics remained silent and said nothing. So many of them inside felt angry, felt hatred, when instead we should have been standing up and proclaiming the truth and the good news of Christ Our Lord. Calling for a change of hearts in the peoples of the world.

There are many bad things happening in the world, and they continue to happen, because by our inaction, we allow evil to grow and grow. Until each one of us and until every Catholic in the world starts to live their faith, in that forgiving love for all things and for all people and proclaiming that to everyone, pain and suffering will continue! When we change and start to live as we are supposed to, the forgiving love and light of Christ will shine so bright in this world that darkness, pain and suffering will flee and paradise will come to earth. It begins not with someone else. It begins with each one of you deciding to live as Jesus calls you to. In that forgiving, loving way of Christ Our Lord because when we start to change, then the world starts to change. It begins with you, not with someone else.

Many Catholics say, "I cannot do anything, I am but one person." In yourself, maybe you are right but if you live in Christ Our Lord, then you can do anything. When you live in His forgiving, loving way, you can move mountains, you can change the world and every one of you can be saints in Heaven, just by living your faith.

The Middle East

Many Christians today around the world, when they look to the Middle-East, tend to look in an unbalanced way. We often look to Arabs and see them maybe as less than us. We see Arab men, women and little children being killed and sometimes think nothing of it because they are only Arabs. We see Jewish men, women and little children being killed and we say, "It is terrible!" What sort of Christian love is that?In Christ Our Lord we have to love everyone equal. Christ loves the Arabs and the Jews equally, the Christians, the Muslims, He loves them all the same. He wants all people to come and live in His full truth of Catholicism but when they do not He never stops loving people. How can we do that? So many times I hear people say, "We support Israel and the Arabs are bad."

People should understand that many of the early saints in the Church were Arabs. Some of the Doctors of the Church are Arabs. So why do we think so badly of them? It seems so strange. We should love them as we love everyone else. We should be seeing them with equal love as everyone else and when any persons or any peoples are oppressed, it is our duty as Christians to stand up for them, whether they are Arabs, Jews, Russians or Chinese or whatever. Sadly today, there is a deafening silence from the people within the Church, the lay people. The Pope is speaking up and saying what is happening in the Middle East is wrong but how many of us are standing up and saying things need to be changed? It is our duty to do so and we must start to do it because until we do, there won't be peace in the world.

The Gift of Healing

One day Jesus said to me, "Come to church," so I went to my local parish church and I stood in front of the Sacred Heart statue and the statue came to life and there was Jesus. He said to me, "Hold My hand." So I held His right hand in my right hand and I prayed an Our Father, Hail Mary and Glory Be. Then all of a sudden, I was in complete ecstasy which lasted for several hours and the Holy Spirit was there with me. He said, "I am filling you with My gifts just as I fill anyone who truly believes." Now I did not know what gifts were, I thought maybe I will go home and I had won the lottery.

This ecstasy was going on and on. I could not stop laughing and crying, I had so much joy. I was working at that time and I had to go and see a doctor for work. I was driving along the road in ecstasy in my car and people were looking in at me. They must have thought I was mad. When I arrived and before I was going in the door, I said, "Oh Lord, please let this stop, I have to go and talk to that man." The moment I stepped through the door, it stopped. When I finished half an hour later and I came out, as I stepped out of the door, it started again. The ecstasy just went on and on and it was wonderful. The Holy Spirit said to me to join a Charismatic group so I found one and I went along.

It was wonderful, people were singing happily and joyfully praising God and people getting up, giving words of prophesy - it was fantastic. After a few weeks, the Lord said to me when they asked for words of prophecy, to stand up and speak. So I went up to the microphone and I spoke for about ten minutes. As I was walking up to the microphone, my legs were shaking, my heart was racing and I felt so nervous, so weak. I said, "Lord, what am I going to say, I do not know what to say." He replied, "Do not worry, I will give you the words." So I got up there and I started to speak, and these beautiful words came from my mouth. As I was listening to myself speaking I thought, this is incredible! Where have all these words come from, it is great!

All of a sudden, people in the congregation started to be filled with the Holy Spirit and were going into ecstasy. People were laughing and crying. Later, after the meeting, many people came up to me and said, "You are wonderful, you are really good. You are so gifted, so graced," and I thought, "Yes, I am great." Then the Lord said to me, "Wait a minute, remember who you are! That is your pride and that is satan, be careful!" Suddenly, I realized how easily satan can deceive me. He puts these thoughts of pride in your mind and when you accept them and think on them, satan takes you away from the Lord. When you start to think on these things, you go down that path, and all of a sudden, you are so far away from God and you look back and think, "How could I be so far from God?" However, if you had stopped it in the beginning, by thinking of Jesus, thinking of His passion, you would not have gone down that path.

When God starts to use people and wonderful things happen other people start to praise you and pride raises up its ugly head inside of you. What people need to remember is it is God who does everything and people should not look up to someone like me who may be gifted in certain ways and think how holy and how wonderful they are. You should think how wonderful God is, because people like me are not different from people like you, it is only what God is doing that makes the difference. Actually I look at you and I think you are the gifted people because it took God coming along and give me a good shake before I started to love Him. So many of you have had this faith all your life and just loved God. A wonderful gift, a gift I never had and how I admire each one of you, the truly gifted people.

So do not ever look up to people who may be like me and think they are better than you. In God's eyes we are all the same. It is important also that as you listen to people who speak, regardless of what gifts or graces they may have, you always check what they say is in line with Church teaching. If it is, listen to it, and if it is not, ignore it because our church teaching, our church, is a safeguard against error. Do not ever forget that, because whatever God will give through people will confirm Catholicism. If it does not, then it is not from God.

A few weeks later, I was in Mass and I was looking around in church and I was thinking, 'well those people are not like the Charismatics'. I thought it is great to be with Charismatics, everyone is singing and having a good time. These people in church at mass, they are all quiet, they really don't know. Then the Lord said to me, "That is your pride again. That is satan working on you. Understand many of these people have been coming to church all of their lives. Many of these people have been making many sacrifices. Many of these people have been living the faith, and just because they do not understand the Charismatic gifts and movement, it does not mean they are not close to God and they are not loved by God".

Once again, I felt so ashamed of myself that I had allowed satan to work on my pride. All of a sudden I realized as you do things for God that evil is always working on you. In me, the greatest weakness I have is my pride. I have such a big head and satan works on that. I pray to God that every day He will humble me so that I can be more like Him. Sometimes He does, and it is very painful.

We all have our weaknesses, and we have to be very careful, because satan knows them. That is why it is so important that when you try to love God, when you try to live the faith, you must always keep your focus on God and pray that you are never distracted. Remember all grace, all gifts come from God, all glory is God's. I used to think that I could glorify God in my life. It is impossible. God is glorified in Himself, I cannot make Him any greater, and neither can any of you. What you can do is allow Him to use you so that His glory is seen through you in the world and when you submit yourself in total obedience humbly to His will, then that glory can be magnified in your life. When you do that, that is when you can say truly - I am Catholic.

Perseverance

Later the Lord asked me to start praying for people for healing. So I began to do it and nothing happened. I thought, "Maybe I got this wrong." The Lord said, "No, just keep praying." So I kept on for months, and nothing happened. The Lord said, "Keep praying for people," and so I did. Then one day I was giving a talk in Perth where I live and there was maybe five hundred people there. As I prayed over them many began falling down on the floor. All of a sudden people were jumping up and claiming healings and cripples walking. Later we found out cancers were healed and from that day healings have always been strong.

Jesus explained to me, what He was calling for was my perseverance. He was testing how strong my faith is. He said it is the same for everyone. If you persevere in your faith, God will pour out His graces and gifts through you because each one of you by your baptism is charismatic. Each one of you is gifted. You just have to persevere in your faith.

Our Lady, Queen of the Cross

One day, Our Blessed Mother appeared before a golden cross. She said she was appearing as Mary, Queen of the Cross. She asked me to get it painted. I did not know any artist, so she directed me to one. It was a woman who could not paint and then one day she had an accident and her hands were badly damaged. All of a sudden she could paint these marvellous religious pictures. I explained the vision that I had and she painted it for me.

A few months after it was painted, Jesus said to me, "Sit and look at the picture." I was sitting there, looking at it, and it looked the same to me, so I said, "I cannot see anything." He said, "Keep looking at it, keep looking." I must have been sitting there for one hour, I think, and all of a sudden, I noticed, in her right hand, the face of Jesus had appeared and in her left hand you may see the Sacred Heart of Jesus. A few days later, the dove of the Holy Spirit appeared at the feet of Our Lady and as time went on various faces of angels and the saints have appeared in the clouds. Recently in the golden cross above Our Lady, the face of Jesus has appeared looking down with His arms stretched out on the cross. It is truly a miraculous picture. Every time I take it to my spiritual director, he is amazed with the new faces that he sees in it.

Our Lady said the Lord would grant a grace through her, as Mary Queen of the Cross if you pray through her and with her to God. It is very simple what you have to do. It is just three Hail Mary's, three Our Fathers and three Glory Be's, and then ask for the grace through Mary, Queen of the Cross.

Someone asked me why pray the Hail Mary's first and not the Our Fathers? Our Blessed Mother said, "You pray the Hail Mary's first to join with me in prayer to the Father, the Son and the Holy Spirit." Later Jesus explained, Our Lady has done so much in her life for God, given so much for God and for us, that the Lord just wants to grant as many graces as He can through her. He encourages me to tell people to pray through and with Mary, Queen of the Cross, and ask for a grace. It seems to be graces for the family.

I will tell you about one that happened. There is a woman in Perth whose daughter was in India getting involved in Hinduism and the mother was really worried because she is a devout Catholic and she kept praying and praying for her daughter to come home. It was very hard to contact her daughter because she was out in the bush of India. She was praying through Mary, Queen of the Cross, and she asked for the grace to be able to contact her daughter and that her daughter would come home. Shortly after she had prayed, the phone rang and it was her daughter saying, "I want to come back to Australia." Some other things happened and she could not get the ticket to her daughter, so she prayed to Mary, Queen of the Cross and miraculously, the ticket got there and her daughter caught the plane and came back.

Our Lady said, "There are graces for families. Encourage people to ask for them…just ask for them."

Difficult Time with Prayer

I often thought the more you pray, the easier prayer would get but it does not seem to be that way sometimes. I was struggling so hard with prayer. It was going on for about three weeks and it was a very difficult time, to say the least. I thought it would never end, there were so many bad things happening. Satan was attacking me emotionally, physically, spiritually and he was attacking my family. I can remember at that time there were some really bad physical attacks where I thought I would die and it was very hard to pray. I never thought I would get through it.

The Lord was only there every so often saying, "Trust Me. Persevere." I asked the Lord, "Do these prayers mean anything? I mean they do not seem to mean anything to me." He said, "Of course they do. It is in these moments that you show the depth of your love of Me. Anyone can pray in the good times but it is in those difficult moments, in those hard moments when you persevere you show how much you love Me and when you come through to the other side, when you get past this, you will find many gifts, many graces waiting for you and for anyone who perseveres."

Sacraments under Attack

Anything that is important, anything that is there to bring us closer to God is attacked by the evil one. So often people are thinking we are praying to Our Lady when we pray the rosary. So often people cannot or will not pray the rosary or are advised not to pray the rosary. There is a woman in Perth whose son was involved in the occult. He wandered in the house in the night time barking and screaming like a dog and doing all sorts of terrible things. She had been praying for him for years and nothing had happened and one day she rang me and asked for prayers. As I prayed with her, Our Blessed Mother appeared and she said, "Tell her to pray the rosary, and as she prays it, to see Our Blessed Mother hang it round the son 's neck, it would become a garland of flowers and to see Our Lady hanging it around the neck of Satan where it becomes a chain to weigh him down."

She did this. Within two weeks, he turned his back on the occult, he started coming to church, receiving the sacraments, and he has been on retreats. It shows you how powerful the rosary is. He still has problems and needs a lot more prayer but this shows you that praying the rosary brought him back to God. No wonder, it is under attack.

It is the same with the Charismatic gifts. They are so powerful and strengthening for us and help bring us back to God and help us come closer to God. No wonder, they are often ridiculed and people say that those Charismatics are mad, jumping around, waving their hands around and singing in strange tongues. However, these charisms are in Holy Scripture and they are from the Holy Spirit, no wonder they are under attack.

The Lord said to me, "Anything that leads in prayer, in Holy Scripture and sacraments to the Holy Trinity is not wrong. How can it be?" He asked me to encourage the prayer groups to pray for each other and support each other and help each other, because what happens often unwittingly, we allow satan in and he fills us with pride, and we think we have got the only way. Any way that leads in prayer and in the sacraments to the Holy Trinity is not wrong and should be encouraged. We should be working together for the greater glory of God and not for the greater glory of men.

It is because the sacraments are so important and Charismatic gifts are so important, the rosary is so important that they are all ridiculed. They are all made fun of. They are all seen as worthless by many but they are all so important. So I encourage you to pray more and receive the sacraments more. It is important in bringing you closer to God and important in healing you and strengthening your life as you wait for the life to come.

Conclusion

I just want to thank God for the time He's given me to speak to you, it truly has been a pleasure for me. I always enjoy sharing that what God has done in my life because He tells me that maybe others will see that God will do similar in their lives if they will turn to Him.

His message is one of love that He loves us all and He wants to forgive us all. Like me, many people believe that God maybe doesn't love them, but that's not the truth. God loves every one of us, even the worst sinner. God wants to forgive every one of us, all it takes is for us to reach out to seek that forgiveness, to ask for that forgiveness, to live in that forgiveness by living with Jesus.

Doing that, life becomes happy, becomes joyful, life becomes what it was meant to be - a God-given gift of love.

God bless you all, please pray for me. Thank you.

4   Talk in an African Radio Station

I would like to talk tonight a little bit about how God has brought me to the Catholic faith and has brought me to understand the power of living in that faith. I was a man who did not believe in God. I did not think He existed. My only relationship with the Church when I was young was to go and steal from it. Then God in His mercy decided to change all that. It began at the age of forty with first an angel and then many saints speaking and appearing to me. They started to explain the truth of Christianity and the truth of God.

The Truth of God

They told me that God is love and if I wanted to live as God had created me to, that I had to try and love and not hate people or be angry with people or reject people or turn away from people. They explained to me that the whole of creation exists in God's love because it comes from God's love and the moment I stopped loving, I stepped outside of what God had created me to be and I stepped outside of all that He had created in love, and in doing so, opened myself to evil.

That is why I had so many problems in my life because I had not lived in His love, I had opened myself up to many evil things. The more evil I accepted, the more and more evil came to me and the more and more I grew in evil but now the saints explained to me that if I decided to change, accept God's love into my life, to try and stop sinning, to pray, to receive the sacraments, to read scripture, to be obedient to the Catholic Church and of course to love God above all others and above all else and to love fellow man, then I could live as I was created to live, live in love, and then my life would become a happy, a joyful, a peaceful one.

Now that is an interesting thing, because when I talk to people about this, when I talk about obedience to the Catholic Church, so many find that hard to accept as I used to in the past. Later, Jesus Himself explained to me that the Catholic Church is the Body of Christ, this is the Church that Our Lord gave to mankind. There was only one Church in the beginning, the Catholic Church and if I wanted to live in the fullness of God's love I had to be a Catholic. That does not mean that God is not in the other Churches, in the Protestant Churches or in any other Churches - He is. However, the fullness of His truth resides only in the Catholic Church.

They explained that if I looked to the early Church, it was obedient and it brought many to sainthood. Many were completely obedient to His love and even gave their lives in obedience to live the Catholic, Christian way. They explained that I needed to live that way today because if I was not obedient, once again I was stepping away from the love of God and in disobedience opened myself to evil, to confusion, to uncertainty. They explained that if I lived in total obedience to the Commandments and teachings of the Church, my life would be clear and I would know where I had to go, what I had to do and how I had to live because it would become obvious.

As I started to do this, it was true. All of a sudden, I saw that if I loved God, surely I would want to please Him, surely I would want to be obedient to His Commandments, to all of them. In the past, I had been selective. I would say, well I agree to one Commandment, and I would be obedient to that, but that other one, I would say, well, I don't want to obey that one, I will ignore it. The Saints explained that if you are not obedient to one Commandment it means you are disobedient. Obedience means obeying all of them and being obedient to the Commandments that Jesus has given us.

Jesus said the two greatest Commandments are to love God and then to love fellow man. Again I saw that if I wanted to please God, I had to do these things. Now I started to love people instead of hate them and it was wonderful because in the past I had been so angry with people but now I could see Jesus in each person and wanted to embrace them and love them and call them brother and sister. Now doing this a peace came within me, a happiness, a joy that I had never known before and now wherever I go in the world, whenever I look at any person, whether they are Catholic, whether they are Christian or they are Muslim or Hindu or Jew, anyone, I see my brother, I see my sister. I see someone who was created in the image of God's love and someone I must love if I love God.

His Body and Blood

I also looked to some of the other Commandments that Jesus gave to us. He said that we should eat of His Body and Blood and that unless we ate of His Body and Blood, we would not have life within us (John 6, 53). The Lord had me go to the Eucharist in the Catholic Church very often. I used to go once a year. Now, seeing this Commandment, it became so obvious to me that Jesus Himself is saying that I had to eat of His Body and Blood. He showed at the Last Supper that His Body and Blood is the Bread and Wine of Communion. Saint Paul confirmed it later in Scripture when he said that if we eat unworthily of the Body and Blood of Christ, then we are liable to condemnation (1 Corinthians 11, 27-29).

Now it became so obvious that this was a clear Commandment of God, a Commandment that would lead me to be united with Him so I could be able to grow more and more like Him in the Eucharist. So now I started going to Mass because I wanted to please Jesus. I did not want to be like those others who turned away and said, in John 6 "How can this man give us his flesh to eat?" "This saying is hard, who can accept it?" How sad it is today that so many people feel the same. So many people turn away and do not believe, yet there it is, in Scripture, plain to see, plain to read, a Commandment from Jesus yet so many deny it and so many do not believe.

As I started to receive the Eucharist in love, I began to feel Jesus filling me, loving me, overwhelming me with His love and changing me to be more like Him. Every Eucharist now seemed to make me want to love more because now I could feel this big love inside of me. It was incredible and I wanted to have more of it. I knew the way to have more of this love was to live as love, and to come to the Eucharist in love, to receive love, divine love...the love of Jesus. As I began to do this, the Lord poured out His love in abundance and began to pour out gifts and graces to me, the gift of healing, and so many people have been healed by the power of God. That power comes from the Eucharist. It comes because I am united with Jesus Christ Our Lord who is truly present in every Mass.

When I receive Him within, I say, "Lord, fill me with Yourself, change me to be like You. Let me die to myself and come to life in You so that You can use me, You can pour out Your holy power, Your divine power to change the world in the way You want," and He does it. The

111

wonderful thing is that He will do that for every person, not only me because He loves each one of you. That is why He said, "Unless you eat of My Body and drink of My Blood, you shall not have life within you," because unless you eat and drink of His Body and Blood, you do not have Jesus completely within you. Jesus who is life, pure life, holy life, divine life…life for everyone.

I encourage you, if you are not going to the Eucharist, to read Scripture, to study it, and look and see what Jesus is saying to you. Ask the Holy Spirit to show you the truth and when He does, accept that truth and come and receive Jesus in the greatest sacrament of all, the Eucharist.

For me, the sacramental life has changed me so much. The more I receive the sacraments, the more I want them because in every sacrament, I feel the presence and the power of God, the love of God. I understand why it is so important in everyone's life, and understanding that, I also understand why they come under so much attack. Anything God gives us to empower us to make us more like Him, to bring us closer to Him, and to live as we are meant to live, evil will attack it. Evil will try and make it seem worthless, as if we do not need it, as if it is not important, because evil does not want us to receive Jesus in the Eucharist, does not want us to receive forgiveness and cleansing in the sacrament of confession and all the wonderful graces and gifts in the other sacraments. It is because there is a treasure there, a divine treasure for every person so evil attacks the sacraments intensely and sadly confuses many people.

That is why I always encourage any person who reads Holy

Scripture to read the words of Jesus and to live to those words, the words of truth, the words of God, the words of life.

God, Catholicism and other Religions

Sometimes people, when they hear me speak and maybe at the grotto today, they think that I would say it was only Catholics that would go to heaven and that maybe Protestants and Jews and Hindus or people of other beliefs are not. That is not what I am saying. What I say is the fullness of God's love on earth resides in the Catholic faith but it is not only Catholics that go to heaven. Many other people can also and it is not all Catholics who go to heaven because you have good ones and you have bad ones just as you have good and bad Protestants and good and bad Jews and Muslims.

God judges people by what is on their heart and the faith that they know. He judges them on that. When Jesus came to me, when the saints came to me, they told me to live the Catholic faith because it is the fullness of God's truth on earth and that is found nowhere else. As I started to do that, I found out that it is the truth but the truth of God also resides in other Churches, but not to the full extent as it does in the Catholic Church. Catholics always should remember that many people who love God are in other Churches and we should never look down upon them and we should never speak badly about them, but we should reach out in love to try and bring them to the fullness of truth so that they can experience the completeness of God's love on earth.

Jesus gave me a vision once when He was explaining the difference between Churches to me, because I said, "There are many good Protestants and they know the Scripture really well and they pray for healing, they have many other wonderful gifts and they seem very good people. I wonder why they have separated from us and we are not together in the goodness of God's love." He explained, "Remember when I walked the earth. There were many synagogues around full of people reading Scripture, praying, praising God, even praying for healing at times. This is how the Protestant Churches are today, full of these good people, reading Scripture, praying, praising God, just as the synagogues were but there was only one place where the Sacrifice happened and that was the temple in Jerusalem. That temple today is the Catholic Church, this is where the Sacrifice takes place, this is where the completeness of faith is, because the Eucharist is present there."

He continued, "Because people in other churches do not have the fullness of truth it does not mean they are bad people. They love God and God loves them." My duty, however, as a Catholic is to reach out to those people and encourage them to understand what they are missing out on, they are missing out on the most important part of their faith, and that is the Eucharist, where you can unite with God, be one with God and find a good life in Him.

Sadly, as I travel around, I hear many people condemning other religions. I hear other religions condemning the Catholic Church and people fighting amongst themselves, all proclaiming to love God. Well, God tells us to love, to love Him and to love each other. So why are we fighting?

Why are we arguing, there is no need for that. We should be united as a force of love in this world, trying to grow in God's love and understand His love better. Uniting together, helping each other to become what we are created to be, images of God on this planet so that His love can spread and change this world to be the paradise it was meant to be.

While we argue, while we have confusion and division amongst us it is no wonder evil is so powerful in the world. When those who love God can unite in His truth, live in His truth and proclaim His truth together throughout the world, then darkness will begin to flee and paradise will come to earth and God's kingdom will be here. It begins with each one of us deciding to live the way Jesus calls us to live, to live in that completeness, the fullness of Him and to be obedient to everything He said to us in the Commandments. If you do that, then truly your lives will change, the country will change, the world will change for the better. It all begins with you, you in Christ, in the Eucharist.

Start reading the Bible

The advice I would like to give is that first of all, if you are a Christian to start reading the Bible and start seeing what Jesus said. What happens is that some people are reading the Bible, and they live to the Old Testament, but that is not Christian. Being a Christian means living the New Testament, living what Jesus said, being Christ-like. Yes, we refer to the Old Testament, but we live the New

Testament, the New Covenant, and that is what being Christian is. So when people look at the New Testament and look at what Jesus said, they must follow that exactly, not make excuses to do different things. Not referring to the Old Testament to change the New Testament but to see the fulfilment of the Old Testament in Christ Our Lord and to live what He said.

One of the main Commandments He gave us is the Eucharist and that is why I spoke about it so much because there is misunderstanding. People do not understand that God has commanded us to receive the Eucharist, and when we deny that, we deny God in our lives, that sadly causes us so much pain.

I would like to thank the Bishop for giving me his time on the radio and thank you all for listening to me. May God bless you, and I ask you to please pray for me. Thank you.

5 Talk to the Sick

My mother comes from Ireland and is a very strong Catholic. She tried to bring me up as a Catholic but when I was very young, I just could not believe. You could not hear God, could not feel Him, not touch Him - or so I thought.

Life got worse and worse and I never thought about God and I just kept doing bad things. I almost killed   several people and I thought if God existed He would not like me. One day, God decided to change my life. It began at the age of 40 when I began hearing a voice speaking to me. I thought I was going mad. The voice told me that it was an angel and that God had sent the angel to me because He loved me and because He wanted my love. Now I did not believe in angels so I tried not to listen, yet this voice kept telling me that God loved me and that He wanted my love. Eventually I said, "If God existed, He would not love someone like me who has been so bad. If He existed, surely He would condemn me to hell." The angel said, "God does exist and He loves you as He does love all people, regardless of who they are or what they do, regardless of the sins they committed. God always loves you and He loves every person. He does not like the sin we commit but He never stops loving us."

He said that when people go to hell, it is because they condemn themselves there, that throughout their life, God is always reaching out, even up to the moment of death, reaching out offering everyone salvation. If anyone goes to hell, they go there by their free choice, by freely rejecting God. The angel said, "God wants everyone to come to heaven," …even me.

In His love, God gives us the free choice to accept or deny His salvation. If anyone does go to hell, it is because they deny their salvation and make their free choice to go there.

Later saint John and other saints explained to me that God is love. Everything that is created is created in love, so if I wanted to exist in the way God had created me to, I must love so that I could experience God's love in each moment. With their help I got the grace to do so. Every moment when I would look at the sun, the moon, the sky, the animals, the grass, or any person, I would see God's love. Every time I breathe in, I feel God's love filling me, every time I breathe out, I feel that love going out to other people. What I found, living that way now, it changed me within, it made me much stronger.

Grace in Suffering

It gave me the strength to carry so much that I had found difficult to carry before, because like many of you, I had some hard times in my life with suffering, sickness and illness. When all of this started happening, I was saying, "Why has God allowed me to be sick? Why me, why not someone else? Why doesn't God heal me?" but as I started to experience God's love in each moment, I realized that the sickness I had and which I still have was a wonderful way of coming closer to Him. As I experienced His love in every moment, when the pain would come, when the suffering would come, the strength and the joy to carry it would be there also.

Then I started to see Jesus suffering and dying on the cross. Now I saw no matter how much I hurt, no matter how much I suffered, no matter how much pain I had to carry, it was nothing compared to what Jesus carried on the cross. At the times where I nearly died and I was in so much agony, still I looked at Jesus on the cross and I saw He suffered more than me. Then I offered my suffering to Him and in return I would get the strength, the joy, the happiness to carry it. So now whenever I get suffering I always try and thank God for it because I see it as a way of coming closer to Jesus.

I saw that if I called myself a Christian which means to be Christ-like, just as Christ Our Lord suffered, then for me to be like Him, I must suffer too. So unlike in the past when suffering used to make me feel so miserable, so angry at times, now it has changed, it makes me feel at peace, it makes me feel a joy within, even though at times I may not look that way. I found also that when you have that change of heart, instead of being miserable and unhappy in your suffering, that if you can find the joy of Christ in your suffering, it makes things much easier.

Often I am around many dying people because I am asked to pray for their healing and there seems to be two types of people. There are those who do not know God in their suffering and so often they are miserable and you don't want to be around them, they make you feel miserable. Then there are those who know Christ in their suffering and they are joyful and they are happy and you just want to be with them because they make you feel so good. In each one of those, truly you see a saint.

I have come to understand that suffering is not a punishment. God did not bring suffering into my life and into other people's lives to punish us. It should not be a terrible burden. However, suffering can be a gift from God that can bring us closer and closer to Him. In our suffering, He actually pours out grace in a powerful way because now we share in the suffering of Christ on the cross.

With the encouragement of the saints I started going to Mass more and more. Before that I used to go once a year at Easter because I wanted to remain a Catholic because I thought when all Catholics die, they go to heaven, so I better be one. So at every Easter I used to go to confession and communion as an insurance. At that time the Mass did not mean anything to me but now I started to go to Mass once a week, twice a week, eventually daily.

One of the first times I went, I was standing outside the church door and it felt as if a hand had taken hold of me and just pulled me inside the church. As I stepped through the church door, that ecstasy I was feeling in prayer, I now felt a thousand times stronger. I could not stop crying, I could not stop laughing, it was wonderful and if I had died at that moment I would have been happy, because I felt so good. I thought life cannot get any better than this.

The priest began to say the Mass, and his words were like electricity, filling the air, filling the church, and each of those words seemed to penetrate my soul and lifted it higher and higher in this ecstasy. Now I recognized that each word of the Mass was sacred, was holy, was filled with the power and the love of the Holy Spirit, and I could feel that power, that love touching me. I just felt as if I would burst open, I was so happy and again, if I had died then I would have been content.

When I received Communion it was like a tidal wave of love washing over me. I experienced the deepest of ecstasies, I experienced emotions I had never known before as I felt the love of Jesus filling me. I knew at that moment that Jesus was present in the Eucharist and I knew He loved me and I knew He wanted me to be one in His love. It was the most wonderful thing as His divine love filled me and seemed to lift me beyond this world.

All of a sudden the things in this world seemed so unimportant. All that seemed to be important now was being united with Jesus in His love. Later He showed me heaven and it was wonderful, complete love and ecstasy which increased and increased. Experiencing every happy moment, every good moment that ever happened throughout time and I knew this is where I wanted to go when I die. I realized this life is but a journey to find our true home. I realized also that if I wanted to find that true home, that the doorway was through Jesus and as Jesus is the Eucharist then the doorway must be through the Eucharist.

So the more I went to the Eucharist, the closer to the path of heaven I would be. The more I went to the Eucharist, the less chance there would be for me to fall from that path. Now I have to go to Mass every day so that I can experience that deep love and deep joy of Jesus in my life. What happened was the more I received Jesus, the stronger I felt inside of me. Jesus said to me later, "Of course you will feel stronger because when you receive Me, you receive My power. The power of My love, and that is what is strengthening you."

All of a sudden these feelings I had before of being unloved, unwanted, uncared for, less than others…all that was taken away from me because now I knew that Jesus loved me and He cared for me and that I was special to Him. He healed me of many things in the Eucharist, He healed me of anger, resentment, of hatred. He healed me of so many bad feelings and He made my life completely happy. When He healed me of those, I did not ask Him to heal me of the other things I had because I felt complete in Him and my physical sufferings did not bother me any more. He healed me in the way that was best for me and that was spiritually.

So now I thank God for anything I get, any suffering, any pain, because I know that spiritually, inside, God has made me good. I know that this body is not the man Alan but that it is part of the man Alan and when my spirit is healthy and shining strong, that this can strengthen my body to endure anything.

Jesus said to me that the Eucharist is the most powerful healing prayer of all. Then He showed me by healing me spiritually in the Eucharist but also He does it physically for many people as well. In the Eucharist, Jesus, the greatest physician, will pour out His healing power to every person who comes seeking it but you need a mustard seed of faith, coming believing in that healing, truly looking for it. In Mass we say, "Only say the word Lord and I shall be healed." Jesus is saying to every person, "Be healed." The problem is that most of us are not listening.

If you come to the Eucharist truly seeking healing from God in the way that is best for you, He will do it because He loves you and he wants to give you what is best for you. So when you come to Mass in future, come saying, "Lord, heal me, heal me." Keep saying it in every Mass. Then one day you will find that you have been healed. It may not be in the way that you wanted originally, but it will be in the way that is best for you. Like me, I know that many of you then will start to experience joy in every moment of your life no matter how bad it is.

Confession

The reason why I am speaking to you about confession and the Eucharist is because these are the most powerful sacraments in which to find healing. Sometimes people come saying to me they were not healed when I prayed with them but when they had a good confession afterwards and they wonder why. It should be obvious to everyone, when you hold on to sin, you hold on to the pain, the hurt, the suffering that comes with it. So how can you expect to be healed when you are holding on to hurt?

Some people do not go to confession at all and they wonder why they have problems in their lives. The reason you often have problems in your life is, the more you hold on to sin and to evil, the more evil puts upon you for that is what evil brings, problems. Some people go to confession and they do not confess everything, they hold back the really big sins because they are ashamed, they are embarrassed, they don't want the priest to know what they are really like.

However, when you do that you are only hurting yourself because all you are doing is holding on to pain. God knows everything about you, He knows every bad thought, every bad feeling, every bad action, even when you are alone and sinning, God is there watching you, there is nothing you can hide from Him. God loves you so much, He gave His life for your forgiveness. He shed His Blood to heal and cleanse your very soul and He will forgive you anything, no matter how bad it is. All He wants you to do is come and ask for that forgiveness, truly repent, and it is there for you.

When you come to confession in that way and confess all your sins, then God cleanses and heals your soul and once your soul is healed, often you are healed physically and emotionally as well.

So if you really want healing, I encourage you, have a good confession and go frequently to the Eucharist seeking healing in every Mass. I promise you then God will touch your life in a special way.

6 Interview

Can you tell us a little bit about your background?

I was born in Bedford, which is North of London. At an early age, I moved to London and stayed there until I was 21. I was born to an English father and an Irish mother from county Kerry. At the age of 21, I migrated to Australia with my wife and we have two adult children, a daughter and a son. I live in Perth in West Australia and I hope to live there for the rest of my life.

Were you born into a Catholic family?

Yes. My mum is an Irish Catholic from the county Kerry who tried to bring me up in the faith but I had no interest. I never prayed, I had no interest in religion at all. I must have caused her a lot of heartache when I was young.

I was a bad guy. I didn't believe in God and God wasn't in my life. I was trapped in the world, I was after money, I was after a good time all the time, addicted to many things, and in those addictions and in that seeking of a good time, I hurt many people by the way I behaved. Also I was extremely violent. So, my life wasn't a good one and God never really came into it by my free choice.

We need to explain that this was kind of a repeat of your childhood, because your father was an alcoholic. It was a similar situation, because you told me you started drinking at age 12!

My father was a violent alcoholic gambler, and I think I imitated him in the violence and the alcoholism, not in the gambling, I never gambled. I saw that when he was violent and aggressive towards people, that many people in London, where I lived at that time, also were frightened of him and they seemed to give him a grudging respect. I thought, the only way I'm going to get respect from people – I don't have any intelligence, and we were very poor -, so the only way I would get respect from people was through violence and through getting lots of money through stealing. So I became extremely violent and was imitating my father in that way, because I had seen the respect that he got from his violence.

I was drawn into the alcoholism as well, because when I started to drink, I would get these good feelings and all the bad things that happened didn't seem to bother me so much, but you know, there was always the next day when you felt worse, so I would drink again to get rid of that feeling.

And you were actually as a child going to churches to steal money out of the baskets or the candelary...

Wherever I could. I did get caught by two policemen in St. Edmund's Church in Edmonton, London when I was stealing out of the candle box, and I had to go before a judge. I would go in a church, I never thought God was there, and there used to be money there, and I needed money, so I took it. I just never thought of God.

So even though you were born into a Catholic family, you weren't brought up practising the faith?

My mum used to try to get us go to church but I never went or very rarely. She used to try to get me to pray but I used to avoid that. She was trying to lead us to the faith and set a good example, but really, I just ignored it completely. I liked to play and get out of the house and caused so many problems and so I never prayed. In the end I think she gave up on me, but of course, she continued to pray for me.

Your family was not the only one, you interacted with other people. So some of your friends were doing the same things that you were doing, is that correct?

We were in a very violent part of London, and most of my friends were gang members and were thieves, as I was. So the group of people that I associated with were similar to me. My best friend murdered someone. Another friend of mine was murdered at the age of 17, another blinded in a fight, another friend of mine tried to murder an older woman, this was the sort of things that were happening in my life.

And you took karate and got the black belt?

I started to do Aikido, because I realized I was quite short, I am 5 foot 7, and there is a lot of big men out there. I realized when the man who was protecting me was put in prison for 12 years for murdering someone, so I thought, I have got to protect myself more. So I decided to study martial arts. I achieved a fourth degree black belt and was Captain of the Australian team in the 1992 World Championships in Tokyo.

One of the things I learnt from that is, that no Christian should really send their children or keep going themselves to martial arts, because all it teaches you is not discipline, it just teaches you to hurt other people, to break their bones, to punch them, to kick them, to even kill them.

And you almost killed two people.

Yes. I had a very bad temper, I was jealous of people, I was angry with people, felt a lot of hatred towards others, because they had what I didn't have, they had money, they had the love of a family – before I got married, I didn't have that. They had what I wanted, and I would get angry, because they had it, and I didn't have it, so I would want to hurt them.

But you had the grace, you had the memory of your mother, so when the time came for you to get married, you had a good picture of the kind of person you would want to marry, is that right?

My mother was always there praying and praying the rosary and trying to be an example. I thought I didn't take any notice, but later on, I realized the good she was doing for all of us. One of the things she seemed to instil in me was that marriage was for life, and when I got married, I just knew that this was it – don't get divorced, you're married until you die, and it doesn't matter what happens in your marriage. You have to make every effort to keep the marriage going. Saying that, I never made much of an effort to keep it going, but I never wanted to get divorced, I never wanted to leave my wife.

You have some brothers. Are they the same as you?

I have four brothers. One of my brothers was in the same category as me, maybe not as bad as me. My eldest brother, we thought, was a religious nut, he used to pray and go to church. But my two younger brothers, by the time they got to the teenage years, life was better, because then, my mother was working full time, 12 hours a day or so, to feed them and bring things in. Life had got better then. So the two younger brothers didn't experience the poverty and the violence that maybe the older ones experienced.

You then met your wife-to-be, and she is from Australia.

I met her and I sort of covered up what I was really like and she didn't see my true self. She saw me drinking a lot, but she didn't realize that I was addicted to the stuff. She must love me. She married me.

I didn't have a good job, I was working in a warehouse and didn't have any education. I got thrown out of school at age 14, because of stealing from the school, a Jesuit school. I was stealing what I could. I had the worst record in the school.

Life wasn't good in England, and I was really struggling, so my wife said, let's go to Australia, life is better there. So I agreed and we went there in 1976. It was easier and it was much better. I can only see God's hand in my life then, because when I got there, by my telling lots of lies and not telling the truth, I managed to obtain this job with a pharmaceutical company, but then, I had to study really hard, once I got the job, so I could keep it. I started studying about medicine and I ended up as a sales manager for one of the companies there. It was a great job, and easy job, lots of money and plenty opportunity to drink and go out and have an exciting time, and I thought I would never leave that job. But when God came to my life, the first thing I wanted to do was quit and just do His work.

Let's talk about how that happened. You were on a business trip...

I just arrived in Adelaide in South Australia and I think it was about 8 o'clock at night, I was sitting on the bed and I was just watching the news. I hadn't been drinking because generally, I wouldn't be drinking throughout the day because of work. So I just got off the plane, got to the hotel, and I was watching the news, then, all of a sudden, before me appeared this man. He began to strangle me. He was dark, his eyes were drawn back, his teeth were drawn back. I didn't take too much notice how he looked like, all I was concerned about was, he was strangling me.

I tried to use my martial arts to stop it, but my hands just went through him, there was nothing I could do and I thought I was going to die, I really did. I felt like I had taken my last breath and I could feel the veins in my neck about to burst. When all of a sudden, I had this voice in my head saying to me, "Pray the Our Father!" And that is the last thing I would have thought about. But, in desperation, I started praying the Our Father. As I prayed, the strangling stopped, so then I stopped praying. When I stopped praying, the strangling started again. This went on all night. Every time I stopped praying, the strangling would start, and every time I prayed, the strangling stopped. I couldn't get out of the room, every time I tried to, this man was just strangling me, I couldn't move, I was trapped. It was a very frightening experience. The next morning, I moved to another hotel. This is how it all started.

What did you think about it? Did you think your mind snapped or anything like that?

I did, because you hear of people who are drinking and they see pink elephants going up the wall, I thought that was me. But then, I saw my neck and I had bruises and I knew it was real. But I wasn't sure what was going on, I was very confused at that time. And confused with this voice in my head that started talking to me.

Did you react to that in any religious way?

Not at all, because at that time, I had no thoughts of God. If I was in trouble, I would say, God help me, and that would be it. Or I would say 20 seconds of prayer at night as an insurance policy, in case I died over night, I had said a prayer and if God existed, He would take me to Heaven, wouldn't He. That was my sum relationship with God. I didn't even think of the Church.

But this voice that encouraged me to pray then told me it was an angel. Now I didn't believe in angels, I didn't believe they exist. This voice told me God had sent this angel because He loved me, He wanted my love. I said, "If God exists, surely He wouldn't love someone like me, I have been so bad, almost killed several people, done all these bad things in my life. Surely He couldn't love someone like me!" However this angel kept telling me that God did love me, God loved every person, regardless of who or what they were, regardless of the sin we commit, God's love remains constant.

He didn't like the sin and the bad things we did, and He called us away from that to live in His love, but God never stopped loving us, and He loved me and He wanted my love. For about three months, that was the messages I was given over and over from this angel, but I didn't really listen.

Then I went back to Perth and I switched on the radio and there was this New Age psychic man on the radio, talking about angels, and I thought, "Oh, I've got to listen to this man." But when I went along I thought, "This man is crazy." So I learnt very early on that this New Age stuff is a lot of rubbish, it was so obvious that it was just wrong.

Did the angel's comments have any impact on your lifestyle?

Not at that time. The only affect was that I was confused and uncertain of what was going on. The violent attacks were continuing and they still happen today, but at the same time I had this voice telling me God loved me and God wanted my love. So I was just uncertain what was happening. You know, maybe I'm going crazy.

Did you talk about this to your wife?

After a short while, I did. She was a bit uncertain at what was happening, and later on, within a short time, she started to believe something was happening, because now, I was changing. I wasn't so angry, I wasn't filled with hatred and I was talking about love all the time, so in the beginning, like me, she was confused, but then, she came to believe.

Can you tell us a little about the time when the angel came into your life?

The first angel that started speaking to me, I presume, was my guardian angel. It never told me, just that it was an angel speaking to me, encouraging me to come back to God. I have seen many of them but there has only been three others that have spoken to me, that's the three archangels, Saint Michael, Saint Raphael and Saint Gabriel. They are often there in times when I am in trouble or when Satan attacks me, so they are there at those times, to help me, to protect me and to guide me. They seem to be there in times of my weakness to give me some extra strength. They are so beautiful and loving.

Sometimes I see them with wings and sometimes I see them without wings, I do not understand that. I do not ask why. My relationship with the Lord is that I very rarely ask Him anything because I believe He knows everything about me. He knows what I need to know and He will tell me what I need to know. So I think it would be wrong for me to say, "Tell me this, explain this to me," because He will know that I need to know this already and would explain this to me. So usually I do not ask any questions, so I do not ask why I see angels with wings or without wings.

When you started speaking to groups, how did that begin?

My archbishop encouraged me to carry on speaking to people, so I started to arrange talks and people started to come along and listen. Many of them would be touched by the Holy Spirit. Many people were finding that the words God was giving me on the sacraments especially were opening them up to a new understanding of the sacraments and helping them to live the sacraments, where before, they had been dead for some people.

You have been out preaching for some time. Have you seen any change at all among Catholics?

Yes, I have. There are more and more young people now looking for God. People seem to be so worried about the young, but actually, lots of young people come to my talks and I see so many of them searching for God. They see the emptiness in the world and they are looking for something else, that something else is God. They just need to be directed to God. So many young people are looking for God and finding faith. Many of the older people as well are starting to live the faith God gave us, not the faith of the world, but the faith God gave us, and they are finding that this is changing their lives for the better and their family's lives for the better. So, there is a change and I think this is the springtime that the Pope has been talking about, and it is starting now. This is the beginning of the springtime, and

I think, in the years to come, it is going to come to fruition in a strong way.

You have a powerful healing ministry, and there have been many healings. In Texas recently, several people were healed, one of them a lady with braces, what about her?

When she came in, I was sitting at the back for Mass, because we always have Mass first, and she was sitting next to me, so I could see exactly how she was. She had braces on her legs and she walked with straight legs, because she could not really bend them. She had braces up her arms and on her hands with this big brace all around her body to hold her straight. She appeared to be in a lot of pain at that time. Then she came up for prayers, and I prayed over her. The next moment she was running up to me saying, "Look, I am healed," and she had all of her braces removed, and I thank God for that.

She just knew she could move because when I prayed over her, as many people do, she felt a tingling through her body. Sometimes, they see a bright light, and sometimes, many are slain in the Spirit. But she wasn't slain in the Spirit, she just had that tingling through her body and the knowledge she was healed. So she just took off everything, and she didn't collapse and she could walk, and it was wonderful.

And there was another woman with cancer who was healed...

She was in the final stage of cancer, expected to die within the next week or two. God is wonderful, He reaches out to people in need. She had the cancer throughout all the major organs in her body, and I think, in the bones as well. I prayed over her, and she went back to her doctor, and they said, the results came back negative, that was a great blessing. That has happened many, many times. God often heals people who are about to die, to bring them back to have a chance to love Him more.

What is the percentage rate of people you are praying over who are healed?

Everyone is affected in a different way. Sometimes, it may be immediately, sometimes it may be a year or two later. We have hundreds upon hundreds of letters of people being healed, but there is only a small percentage of them who write to us.

I was in Washington DC, and there was a blind man who was healed when I had been there the year before. I said, "Did you write and tell me?" He said, "No, I didn't think to." The percentage that are healed I wouldn't know. Physical healings don't happen to everyone, but there are many spiritual healings where people find the love of God in their life renewed. Or if they have never had it, they just discover it and this changes their whole life and brings an emotional or maybe a mental healing.

I couldn't give you a percentage, but everyone is touched in some way. I was up in Toronto for World Youth Day in 2002, and I was in the cathedral there. A man from Iowa came up to me asking, "Are you Alan Ames?" And I said yes. He was there with his teenage son who was about 19. He said, "Two years ago, we came to one of your talks. We came for a physical healing, but we didn't believe in God.

You prayed over us and we fell in love with God. So here we are, at World Youth Day. We love God." – For me, that was fantastic.

What is it that you tell people in your talks?

Sometimes the talks are very similar but sometimes they are completely different. They cover just about everything in life and we have the healing that follows. Usually what you will find is by the end of the talk and the healing prayers, there are many healings that occur spiritually, physically and emotionally. Often you see people who come in and they look very sad, very depressed, when they leave, it is like they are walking on air because the Holy Spirit touched them and filled them. That is what brings me great joy to see people change in this way.

You mentioned people could get healed during the talk itself. Can you explain that?

During the talk itself, often people are healed. In Texas recently, a young deaf boy was there with his mother and as I was speaking, he said to his mother: "Can you tell this man to speak a bit quieter because He's speaking so loud." He was hearing for the first time and I thank God for that. Then the healing continues with prayers after that. Sometimes people are a bit uncertain about these prayers because I may pray in tongues and sometimes there are people falling down in the Spirit and if you have not seen that before, it's a bit of a shock.

Do you have the gift of tongues?

Yes, I do. The gift of tongues is very special. I find when I pray in tongues for myself, if I am feeling a bit down, it just lifts me. Also it just happens spontaneously in healing. Some people are frightened when they hear tongues, but it is from the Holy Spirit and it is in Holy Scripture. It is nothing to be frightened of. So if you hear me praying in tongues, do not be shocked or frightened. Just realize it is from the Holy Spirit.

Many people wonder what Praying in Tongues is.

Praying in tongues is praying from your spirit to God, expressing your love for Him. What I find is when I run out my human words to say, all of a sudden I flow into tongues and I feel this warmth inside of me, I feel my love reaching out from my soul to the Father, Son and Holy Spirit and it comes out in these words that sometimes I understand and sometimes I do not. They have been in various languages, they have been in German, in French, in Arabic, languages which I don't speak but they just seem to flow out and often people have interpreted them, Polish once. So when you pray in tongues, it is nothing to be frightened of, it's your spirit expressing your love for God. Sometimes when we pray in tongues and it comes out in different languages, this is for people who are in the congregation to give them a message in their language so they can understand that God is speaking directly to them.

I remember there was a Polish speaking woman in Australia and as I was praying in tongues, it came out in Polish. Now I do not know any Polish. There was a message for this woman which was to comfort her and to strengthen her. The woman came up to me afterwards and said: "I could understand what you were saying, it was Polish." She did not know why she was getting that message but the following week her brother died in a mine accident where the mine collapsed. So what was happening was, the Lord was preparing her and giving her messages of love and support to help her through that time and it really did because she knew then that God was with her in that difficult moment.

So sometimes, in the tongues, the Lord is giving messages to people. It is a gift of the Holy Spirit and these gifts are all in scripture and they are from God and we should not be afraid of them.

When you pray with people, some get slain in the Spirit. Many people are afraid of that.

When people are slain in the Spirit, often there's a lot of fear about that. You see people falling down and think, what is happening, have they passed out? Sometimes the Holy Spirit works in that way. What He seems to do is, He puts people down so to take their minds out of the way so that He can do what He wants to do without any interference from us. It is always a wonderful experience, a joy-filled experience which touches people deeply and sometimes changes their whole life.

It is part of the healing process but it is not essential. Sometimes when I pray over people, just about everyone falls down, and at other times, hardly anyone falls down. Sometimes it is in between. In the beginning I used to be a bit worried about that, I thought why are not people falling down? The Lord said, "They do not need to. The important thing is that you pray with them, and if I want to put them down, I will, and if they do not need to be put down, I will not." So sometimes He does and sometimes He does not but the healings are always strong. Some people resist when they are being prayed over and I see them really struggling, trying to stop themselves falling down. Now, that's like coming to God saying "Lord, please heal me!" Then, as He touches you with the Holy Spirit, saying, "Oh no, I do not want it!" If you say no, you have that free choice and of course, then God may not heal you.

So I always encourage people that if God touches them in that way, do not resist, do not be frightened, accept that healing. If He does not touch you in that way, do not think He is not healing you because He is just working in another way in you. People may think if someone falls down and they do not themselves, the person who went down is holier than them. That is not the case at all. It just means that God is working in another way in that person. So, the slaying in the Spirit or resting in the Spirit is nothing to be afraid of, it is a wonderful experience, it is part of the healing process but it is not essential.

Is the phenomena of being slain in the Spirit something new, or did it also exist in the early Church?

First of all, when Jesus prayed with people, some of them fell down. If you read Holy Scripture, you will see that. Also, it is approved of by the Church, the Church agrees with it, it is not against Church teaching. So, as a Catholic, we have to accept that. What we have to avoid is the hysterical events where people get pumped up and get excited so that their mind does it, and not God.

Let's talk about the value of your crucifix and why you use this one to pray with people.

It is a Benedictine crucifix, and they are very powerful. This particular crucifix bled in 1995 from the crown of thorns and left shoulder and later, for almost two years, it was weeping fragrant oil that smells of roses. When we took a photograph once of the oil, the face of Jesus appeared on the back of the crucifix. So, it is a very blessed crucifix. All crucifixes are blessed, but for some reason, God seems to be doing a lot with this one.

Of course, it is Jesus who is doing the healing, and when I use the crucifix, it reminds of the sacrifice of Jesus and the power of His healing through His sacrifice.

We had the oil tested in the university of New South Wales in Sydney, Australia. The results came back as olive oil with a fragrant essential oil which they couldn't identify, and for them to not be able to identify that oil, is unusual.

Do you use that oil for healing powers as well?

What was happening was, when I was praying over people with it, oil was coming out, and they would be getting it on their forehead . I gave some to people, but I look at it this way: I put the crucifix on their head, and if God wants to put oil on them, He does, and I leave it up to Him.

And the prayers that you pray, that is what God told you to say?

Yes, I mean, I pray in tongues sometimes. I just open my mouth and say the prayers that come out. Then I try to focus on the name of Jesus, the name of the Father and the name of the Holy Spirit, because that is where all the power comes from. Also, in doing so, I think it brings people to focus on God more and not to focus on me. So when I am praying with them I am talking about God as I am praying, it hopefully is bringing them spiritually to reach out to God, rather than thinking, Alan Ames heals them, because I don't do it, it is God who does it.

Why did God give you this healing power?

He said, everyone is hurting in the world. There is no one who is not hurting. Everyone is hurting in one way or another, spiritually, physically, mentally, emotionally. It is so true. I have met so many people, and they are all hurting in some way. God said, what He wants to do, because He loves us, is to take this hurt away and in taking that hurt away, He wants to bring us to Him. So that we can truly come to live completely in His love and be happy, because in the love of God, there is only happiness, joy and contentment.

Our Lord said, when he walked the Holy Land, it was the healing that brought many people to Him, then they would hear His words. But first, many of them came, because they had heard of the blind seeing, cripples walking and the dead rising. So they came and wanted to be healed. In coming for the healing they listened as He spoke to them and gave them His holy words which converted the souls of so many.

So, it is a similar thing, because it is imitating Christ. We have the Mass where Our Lord is, first at every healing service, so that people will see Jesus and receive Jesus within, if they are Catholic. After Mass I speak and the Holy Spirit pours out His grace and touches their hearts and souls. Actually, as I speak, sometimes people are being healed. I remember once a woman saying to me in Minnesota, as I was giving my conversion story and speaking about what the Lord was giving me about the sacraments, she felt all the pain just being lifted from her. All of a sudden, she could stand up which she had not been able to do for a long time. So, often through the talk, people are being healed.

Then, we have the Blessed Sacrament exposed, and I pray over people, so again, it is Jesus there, and people will be focussing on Jesus, and His holy Eucharistic power is pouring out to touch these people. Then, we have priests for confessions so that people can go and have their souls cleansed and healed in that powerful sacrament by the Holy Spirit.

The whole thing about the healing, apart from healing people physically, is to bring them to the fullness of God's love. And the fullness of God's love on earth is Catholicism, and so God wants to bring people through healing to live fully in His love, whether they are Catholics who are not living their faith fully, whether they are Protestants who don't know the fullness of Christianity, whether they are Jews or Moslems or Hindus... We have had Moslems convert to Catholicism.

I remember I was giving a TV interview in Melbourne in Australia, and the cameraman was a Moslem. As he was filming me, the Holy Spirit touched him and later he became Catholic. That was wonderful.

I know it is ideal for people to become Catholic, but is it absolutely necessary?

It is not. The whole thing is to bring people to the fullness of God's truth. If people, say, they are Protestant and they are not Catholic, I mean, they still love God and God loves them. He loves them as He loves Catholics. He hopes that they will come to accept the fullness of His truth, but if they don't, it doesn't stop Him loving them and wanting to heal them It doesn't mean they are bad people.

When I was at the World Youth Day at Toronto, when I was speaking in one of the halls there, it was an Anglican woman who was in charge of it. She had been sick for more than 20 years, couldn't walk properly with a bad back. One of the people who was helping me brought her up for prayers, and I just said a brief prayer with her – she was healed immediately. She couldn't believe it. She said, "A Catholic has healed me, it is wonderful!" From there, I went to Ghana in West Africa where I was giving a talk at Our Lady of Fatima Shrine. A big shrine, thousands of people came along, but amongst those thousands of Christians, there was a Moslem man who had been bleeding for years. He had this bleeding disease and he was coming to the end of his life because he had been bleeding so much, and they just couldn't cure him. I prayed with him, and he stopped bleeding immediately. Then for weeks, he has been running around telling people, a

Catholic has healed him – of course, it was God healing him.

To me, again, what it shows is that God loves all people. He healed an Anglican, He healed a Moslem, He has healed Catholics, Jews, Hindus…He heals everyone, because He loves everyone. So there are no restrictions on people.

How did you get to World Youth Day?

The organisers invited me, and then I was told the Vatican approved all the speakers, and it was quite a blessing for me to be invited to speak at a Papal event. I was blessed to give three talks, and for me, that was a wonderful, wonderful thing, just to be there where the Pope was speaking.

How did you get to Africa?

I often get letters of invitation of poor countries. I try and spend time in the Third World, because they are in so much need, the poor people suffer so much and very rarely do people go there to pray with them for healing or to speak to them. God has blessed me greatly to allow me to do that, so I try to go to Africa quite a lot, and to Asia, to pray with the poor and sometimes to help them financially, if we can. We built a hospice recently in Kenya for people dying of Aids.

All those letters you get about healings, I bet there must be some beautiful stories about spiritual healings as well.

There are so many, and they say, "Look, I never knew God, or I have been away from the Church for 30, 40, 50 years, and I came to your talk, and I couldn't stop crying, because I realized God did care for me…" And they have massive conversions.

One that really sticks in my mind was during one of the first talks I gave in Australia, there was a young man of about 26. He is a rugby player, big and muscular. He was there for the talk and for the prayers afterwards. Then I noticed, afterwards he was sitting there crying his eyes out. So I went up to him asking, "Are you okay?" he said, "For the first time in my life, I know God loves me." He just couldn't stop crying. To me, that was wonderful.

What are the concrete changes, would you say, in your day to day life from the moment of your conversion?

One of the good things is that my marriage has been strengthened. My children have become more part of their family. In the past, my life was a self-centered one and I hurt my family so much, but now we are actually living as a family. When I say living as a family, we actually started loving each other and caring for each other. My marriage has grown so strong. My children's lives are changing so much.

In the beginning, when God came to me, I felt I had to keep telling them about God and force this upon them but the Lord said to me, "Don't do that. The way to do it is to live your life as an example of My love and to take My love into your family. In every moment, try and share My love with your family by the way you live, by the words you speak, by the love you express in everything you do." So I started to do that and it changed my family.

My children thought I was crazy, what with God speaking to me and angels and saints and my wife was a bit uncertain in the beginning. All that has changed. My wife, who was a Protestant, has become a Catholic. She was filled with the Holy Spirit once for seven hours in complete ecstasy, truly wonderful, truly blessed by God. These are some of the things that God told me would happen. He said, "If you step out in My love and always be gentle and always be kind and try not to force My will upon others, bring it to them in a loving way then their hearts will open. It may be a slow process but they will open and then they will be filled by the Holy Spirit."

He said it is the same for everyone. Not only your immediate family. He said, "Remember, the whole world is your family and wherever you go, whoever you speak to, whoever you are with, always express love to them. Show My love in everything you do and in that way you will melt hearts, you will take away the hardness and I will pour My love deep inside".

. Understand also, that each time you receive the Eucharist, when you receive God within, that you are filled with Him, filled with His love, and it is overflowing inside you. In the Eucharist, you can find the strength to take His love to your family, to your friends, to everyone. You can be an imitation of Mary through the Eucharist, just as she went to her family, Elizabeth, in need. Mary took Jesus, who was within her, to Elizabeth and Jesus reached out from inside

Mary to touch Elizabeth and John the Baptist in her womb and filled them with the Holy Spirit. That is what God will do through us. When we receive Him in the Eucharist and allow Him to fill us with His love and then we take that to our family, not only our immediate family, but the family of mankind and allow God to reach out from within us by expressing our love, showing our love to everyone we meet. Through that He will reach out and touch them, touch their very souls and fill them with the Holy Spirit as He has done with my wife and He starts to do with my children.

Are there things like television or drinking that have been eliminated from your life?

Yes. I stopped drinking immediately. One day I was addicted to drinking and the next day I had stopped, by the grace of God. Anyone who has been addicted to alcohol will know how hard that is to do but when I started praying, all my addictions just fell away from me, and now I am addicted to the love of God, and it is the best addiction of all. Television, I watch the news and documentaries and some other things on TV. Often people today say you should not watch it. Television is like anything, it can be used for good or it can be used for bad. Now, in places like America there are Catholic TV networks that bring beautiful messages to people through television. These are the things they should be watching. Also there are educational programmes, such as documentaries that you can watch and learn so much from. So, I watch a bit of TV, but I don't see anything wrong with it. Where it goes wrong is when you watch those programmes that are full of sin, full of filth and swearing and violence.

These are the things we should be complaining against, we should be standing up against. Today many Catholics say there is all that bad stuff on TV and in the newspapers but how many people write to the TV stations, how many people write to the newspapers, how many people stand up and say, "This is wrong! I do not agree with this and I do not want this." Most people sit back and do nothing except complain, and nothing changes. Then what happens is in our apathy we allow sin to grow. We may sit there and disagree with it but if we do not stand against sin, in our apathy we are allowing sin to grow, and it is partly our fault that sin is spreading in the world. What God calls us to do in His love is to stand against sin and not be frightened to do so.

Today many people are frightened because they think they will be ridiculed, people may make fun of them, they would be called crazy. However, the early martyrs in the Church did not take notice of that. They stood up. They gave their lives so that this faith could be spread around the world, the truth could be spread against all the evil in the world. Sadly today we let those martyrs down because many of us, including myself, sit back at times and do nothing and watch evil grow. All we do is we complain and blame other people. We blame anyone else but ourselves. What we have got to do is start looking at ourselves, start living our faith. That is what God calls us to, to live our faith, to stand against sin, and not to do it in a condemning, judgmental way, but to do it in a loving, a kind, a forgiving and a sacrificing way, because that is the way of Jesus.

So today there are many things that are bad on TV and in the newspapers but unless we stand up as a force of God's love against them, then this is not going to change.

Can you share a little about the life of prayer within your family?

Family prayer is very important. I can remember a priest once said, "A family that prays together stays together," it is so true. There are many families around the world who keep praying and they are strong, strong in love. There are other families that do not and you can see the weakness in their families. To me, one of the greatest pains in my life is I never knew God before, so I did not encourage my children or wife to pray when the children were young, so they missed out on that. Now my wife and I pray together and my wife has become a very strong Catholic. I have just heard that my daughter has started to pray, my son carries a rosary with him, and I am sure he is praying it at times. It is a gradual process.

Family prayer, though, I hope will become strong in our house and in the future that together, the four of us can pray together, because as we do, as any family will, then the love within that family will grow and bind them together. As it binds the family together the life of each person in that family will change, they will become peaceful, content, happy people, and they will take that happiness to everyone else they meet. Other people will be drawn and attracted by this love of God in them that is growing through prayer and it is this attraction of God's love to others that will bring others to come to know God. Prayer is one of the foundations, with the other foundations of the Sacraments and Holy Scripture, and I think these should be the foundation of families, because if your family is built on these, it is going to be a strong family. We have to encourage family prayer as much as we can. Whether it is the rosary, Divine Mercy chaplet or the saying of some Our Father's or Hail Mary's together or just sitting quietly together and praying. Whatever type of prayer it is to God, we should encourage that, because it is by prayer that families will change, that families will become united and the terrible problems that we have in families today will disappear.

Jesus and Mary have also shown you some new kinds of prayer. Can you tell us something about that?

There are two rosaries that I was given, one by Jesus and one by Our Lady. I will share Our Lady's one with you. It is called the Trinity Rosary. Our Blessed Mother asked that we pray eleven Our Father's, meditating on God the Father. She explained that so often the Father is forgotten but now as you pray these eleven Our Father's, thinking of Him and thinking of His love which is in your life and in His creation all around you.Remembering every breath you are taking is from His love, created in His love, from God as a gift to you, then you become open to see so much more as you meditate on the Father. All of a sudden things become clear around you, the gifts and graces that He gives you in every day life and how much He loves you.

Then in the Glory Be, again thinking of God the Father in the Holy Trinity.

Next eleven Our Father's thinking of Our Lord, Jesus, how much He loved mankind, how much He gave, how much

He continues to try and bring us back to God.

Then in the Glory Be, thinking of Jesus in the Holy Trinity.

The next eleven Our Father's, thinking of the Holy Spirit, the power, the actions, the graces, the gifts of the Spirit. What the Holy Spirit offers us. The strength He wants to give us.

Then in the Glory Be thinking of the Holy Spirit in the Holy Trinity.

Finally, praying a Hail Holy Queen.

Our Lady said when you pray this she will be praying it with everyone, that she loves to hear people pray this because now you are thinking of the completeness of God, you are thinking of the Father, the Son and the Holy Spirit, the One True God.

She said so often today God is fragmented. People may think of the Holy Spirit if they are charismatic or they may think of Jesus, and often the Father gets pushed to the background. Sometimes the Holy Spirit gets pushed to the background and people focus on Jesus. Well, God is one and God is three and we must think of the completeness of God and meditate on the completeness because when we do that, then we start to live a complete life in God. We must not just see God as one part of the Trinity but we must look at Him as three and as one. When we start to do that, it brings Our Blessed Mother joy because now we are starting to see the complete truth.

Often when we only look at one part of the Trinity it is common to ignore another part and sometimes in that ignoring of another part, the evil one can be there to blow this up and I have seen at times people who say that Charismatics are mad because they are dancing and jumping around, waving their hands in the air and all these charisms they seem to be a bit crazy. People should see these charisms are given by the Holy Spirit and if we had the completeness of the Holy Trinity in our life, a complete understanding of the three who are God, then we would not feel this way about charisms, about the charismatic movement and charismatic people. We would accept it, embrace it, because we would know it comes from the completeness of God.

So, if we have focussed just on one part of the Trinity we leave ourselves open to evil, we become a little bit weak. We can see this effect in other religions where they focus only on the Father, ignoring the Son and the Holy Spirit or who believe God is one not three in one. All people should focus on the wholeness of God, the completeness of God, and that is the Trinity who is the one true God.

There are also some books available connected with your experiences. Can you say something about "Through the Eyes of Jesus"?

'Through the Eyes of Jesus' are three beautiful books. When I was given them at times I was crying and at times laughing they are so beautiful. The Lord gave them to me in a way that I would be looking through His eyes. Sometimes it was like being in a movie screen and it would be happening before you. He allowed me to perceive some of His thoughts and some of His emotions. He shows us His humanity and His divinity. He shows us in His humanity how we can overcome our weaknesses, our fears, our disbeliefs. He showed us how He walked through all the things that were there to tempt Him, to frighten Him or distract Him. He just walked past them in love and showed we can do the same.

He shows over and over that His forgiveness is for everyone. He shows over and over how He wanted to save Judas but how Judas kept rejecting His forgiveness, His love. The Lord shows us in a special way how we can change our lives to truly become imitations of Him in the little things and also in the large things. We see how we can live every day as Jesus wants us to by looking to His life as an example to follow. They are truly beautiful books. They are truly books of conversion. Give it to those who do not know God.

When I got the three volumes it was very exhausting and each one of them took me about three weeks to write, which is not very long. At the end of each two or three hour session when the Lord was giving me some each day, I would be completely drained. When I finished the last volume and the last page and the Lord told me that was the end I felt so relieved because I was so drained but at the same time I was so sad because the words in the books are so beautiful, so simple, so profound, and I thought, isn't it sad that we do not get anymore of this.

'Through the Eyes of Jesus' has had such an effect on people. People who have had no faith and read these books find them so easy to read and there have been many conversions. They are given in such a simple way that anyone can read them. Usually when they start to read them people do not want to put them down, they are just drawn deeper and deeper into the words that God has given and these are beautiful words.

How did you get them?

I was writing it as I was getting it. It is very hard to describe if you have not experienced it yourself but it was as if I was inside Jesus' body, looking out through His eyes, experiencing what was going on, what He was feeling, seeing and hearing, all the conversations and actions that were happening. At the same time, He was giving me the words to write down, so it was all happening at once.

Now Jesus has something else for you to write.

Oh yes, I write every day. I get several messages to write down each day. I write probably down maybe 70% of what I get. The relationship I have with the Lord, Our Blessed Mother, angels and saints is that they are with me all day long. I have constant conversations with them just as I have conversation with you. Some of the things I write down are what they ask me to or I feel inspired to and some personal things I do not write down like when the Lord is telling me He loves me over and over, so I stopped writing that down. It has been there all day and every day now for years.

When the Lord or Our Blessed Mother or the angels or the saints are not there, the other one is there… the evil one, so it is a fine balance between Our Lord and the other one but it is all day and every day. The Lord tells me as long as I continue to lead a sacramental, a prayerful, a scriptural life in complete obedience to His Church, to the Catholic Church, then this will continue.

Has there been any particular experience that has struck you in a particular way?

There are so many. One on Good Friday when I was sitting in the church and I saw Jesus before me on the cross suffering and dying. He lifted me on the cross with Him and I was there again as if I was inside Jesus and I was feeling the pain and the suffering. I came to understand that every breath He took was painful, every movement He made was painful, it was complete agony on the cross. When He put His head up, the thorns would dig into the back of His head when the cross pressed on the thorns. So He would lean His head forward and when He did, His body would tear on the nails. Each breath He took, His body started to tear at the nails, it was just continuous agony. As He laid His back against the cross, His back would be in agony from the scourging and so He would lean forward again and be in agony again as the nails tore on His hands and feet. So, it was continuous suffering.

In that suffering I also felt this deep joy, this deep happiness as I saw Jesus looking out across the world, looking out across everyone and the joy of those who would be saved by His sacrifice. So I came to understand at that moment as well that in this deep suffering that the Lord had, there was this deep joy. Now often when He shares His pain with me, there is this joy as well. It is a very strange experience to be hurting so much at times but to feel a deep joy, a deep peace. So I learnt much from the experience and I will never forget that.

When you go to other continents to give talks, isn't this dangerous sometimes?

I was in Soweto in South Africa where when you stop the car at the traffic lights, they shoot you dead. If a white person walks the street, they shoot you dead, and not only white people, but other people as well. I was walking the streets of Soweto, it didn't bother me, God is with me, He sent me there and He keeps me safe.

Also, I go to lots of the children with Aids in Africa, and the older people dying of Aids, and they are in end stage Aids, they can be bleeding or weeping all over the place. When I first did that, I said to the Lord, "I'm going to get Aids if I do this!" He said, "Look, trust Me. These people need love, they don't need rejection, they are getting rejection from most people. They need love, they need caring. Reach out and embrace them."

So I embrace them, I kiss them, I hug them, they bleed over me, they sneeze over me. I just love them. I don't get Aids but if I do get it, well, that is God's will. I have got to show Christ to these people. I have got to show love to them, and I have not got to be afraid of anything. I hope, by the grace of God, I can remain unafraid.

*Have Jesus and Mary spoken to you about Heaven,
purgatory and hell?*

Oh yes, they tell me that Heaven, hell and purgatory are
the only truth after death. Anything else is a deception.
Today, so many are deceived. All the deceptions of course
come from the evil ones in hell. Heaven is there and I hope
everyone reaches there. It does exist. It is a wonderful,
wonderful place. The Lord has shown it to me three or
four times. It is very hard to describe because I am in
complete ecstasy when I go there. How to describe
complete ecstasy? How to describe when an angel or a saint
touches you? This ecstasy increases and increases. How to
describe when Our Blessed Mother puts her arms around
you? You just feel so full of joy, full of love, it is just an
incredible experience. You think you just cannot feel any
happier than that, it would be impossible, and then Jesus
touches you, and you just explode, you just feel like
bursting. You never want to leave, you just want to be there
forever. The Father and the Holy Spirit are there and it is
just complete joy and happiness. How to describe that is
just impossible to put that into words. Heaven is a
wonderful, wonderful place, I hope everyone goes there.

I used to be so frightened of purgatory, I had this deep fear
of going to purgatory. Now I would really be glad of going
straight in there because I have come to understand that if
you go to purgatory you know you are going to reach
Heaven. So if I could just make it to purgatory I would be
really happy with that; I still have a long way to go.

Purgatory is there, it does exist and there is a reference to
it in Scripture that many people are unaware of. When the
Lord said in Holy Scripture (Mathew 5, 26 and Luke 12,

59), "You will be thrown into prison until you pay the last penny," well, this is what He is talking of…this is purgatory. In purgatory you go there and you atone for the sins that you have committed in your life. Heaven is pure love and sin cannot exist in Heaven so if you committed sin and not truly repented and not been forgiven, then it is impossible when you die that you can go straight to Heaven. That sin has to be cleansed from your soul and that is what purgatory is, where your soul is cleansed when you atone for these sins.

I cannot explain all about purgatory to you because I am under instruction not to, but the little bit I can share with you is that it is very similar to what the Lord showed me when He came to me. There you see over and over all the things you have done in your life to offend God and you see how they hurt God. The pain from that is so intense and you see this over and over until you have atoned of your sins and then God lifts you to Heaven.

Hell does exist, I hope no one goes there. It is a terrible, terrible place. I pray no one ever goes there, even the worst person in the world I do not want to go to hell, I pray for them that they do not. I cannot describe hell to you because I am under instruction not to, but it is a terrible place. Please pray that no one goes there. It is terrible suffering beyond your wildest imagination.

I pray that most people will go to purgatory, the Lord tells me they do, He shows me the majority of people go to purgatory and then they go on to Heaven. Of course, many do go to hell but it is not as many as we believe do because God's mercy is endless, His forgiveness is unlimited. It is only us humans who at times think so many people have been condemned to hell and we forget the mercy of God. What God wants of us is that we pray and pray and offer the sacraments that all those who are living bad lives, who are in mortal sin, who are deceived by evil, that they come to see the truth. He also calls that we should be living our faith and living our faith means to show His love, His forgiveness, His kindness, His understanding and reaching out to those in need, not turning away from them. It is so easy today when you see people doing wrong to turn away from them, to reject them but of course what you are doing is you are not helping them to overcome the problems in their lives. You are just allowing evil to take them further and further away from God. It is your duty as a Catholic, as a Christian, to turn to those who are in need and that means all those sinners out there. Of course we are all sinners, but the really bad ones need you to turn to them and to help them as much as you can, not judging them, not condemning them, just loving and forgiving them.

You said how evil spirits can interfere with our day to day life. Can you say something to clarify that?

There are evil spirits and we should not be blind to that. Often people do not believe that satan or evil spirits exist and of course that is a cunning trick by satan because if you do not believe he exists and there is no hell, you can do what you want in your life. There is no punishment, so what a trick that is! The evil spirits are there, always there tempting us, trying to draw us into sin, trying to frighten us, take us away from God, because when we have fear we start to close our heart a little bit to God. They are there all the time constantly working on us and working on us to try and bring us further and further away from God.

When we pray and we get so many distractions, often it is them. Often they put thoughts on your mind that will draw you into thoughts of your family, your friends, whatever will draw you away from thinking about God. They will do anything to stop you praying, to stop you receiving the sacraments, to stop you loving God, to stop you loving fellow man. So often we see people in need and Jesus calls us to love everyone but often we see people like drug addicts or beggars on the street and we turn away from them. We get these thoughts about how bad they are, how evil they are, aren't they terrible. Looking at the state they are in, we feel superior to them. These thoughts are prompted often by the evil ones and in our weakness, where we go wrong, is that we follow these thoughts, we go down this path and we get led deeper and deeper into these thoughts and deeper and deeper into prideful sin.

What we have to do right in the beginning when we start to get into these bad thoughts about other people, these bad feelings, is to look at Jesus on the cross suffering, seeing He did that for everyone. For these people you are feeling bad about, He did it for them as well and when you focus on that, you will see these bad thoughts will disappear, that evil cannot stay there then. So what I do, because I get these thoughts, I focus on Jesus. The Lord said to me, "Always look to Me, ignore evil. Always look to goodness, always look to God, look past evil. When you focus on evil, you allow it to grow in your life. "

When you look to evil, when you are attracted by it, you allow it to grow in your life. When you pay it any attention, you allow it to distract you from God. He said, "Ignore evil, walk past it and always look to God."

He ignored evil in the forty days in the desert. He showed us clearly, we have to do the same. Ignore evil, take no notice of it, look past it and look to God. The more attention you pay to evil, the bigger it will get. Always look to God, always look to goodness and have no fear.

Today, many people are frightened of evil and frightened of satan and the other evil ones but there is nothing to be frightened of. As Catholics we believe that Jesus has defeated evil on the cross. So we have to embrace that and accept that and trust in that. There is nothing to fear. It is only our doubts, our weaknesses, our disbelief that allow evil to do anything to us. If we hold on firmly to the victory of Jesus then satan cannot harm us in any way at all unless God allows it to happen for our spiritual growth or to pour graces out upon the world.

I would like to share with you one thing that happened to me in Rome. I was staying in the American Franciscans convent which is close to Saint Peter's. I thought I would be safe there. This was not long after the physical attacks had started by satan on me. I thought, "I am on holy ground, I am in a convent, opposite Saint Peter's, nothing will happen here, I will be safe." I woke up at 2 o'clock in the morning and satan was there strangling me. I thought: "This is it, I am going to die." I could feel the veins on my neck almost bursting, my back was arching, it seemed I had not breathed for ages, probably a couple of minutes that seemed like hours. I thought: "This is it, I am going to die," so I said to Jesus, "If this is Your will I accept it. I give You my soul. Look after my family."

The moment I said that, the attack stopped and any time there is a physical attack on me and I feel like I am going to die and I think it is my last moment, every time I say to Jesus and I mean it, "I love You, I give You my soul, and if this is Your will, I accept it," the attack always stops. The reason is because I am completely trusting in Jesus, trusting in His victory and allowing to happen in my life whatever He wants, not what I want, and not allowing my fears to grow. I am just trusting completely in God that His will be done in my life. When people do that, then satan, evil can not harm you in any way. That is what God encourages me to do always, to give myself completely to Him, trust completely in Him and have no fear. There is nothing to be frightened of in this world. Satan tries to make us afraid of everything. If we trust in God, if we call ourselves Catholics and believe truly in the victory of Jesus, the power of the Father and the Holy Spirit, we have nothing to be afraid of. Satan is defeated. Evil is beaten. It is only our fears and our weaknesses to keep it alive in this world.

You mentioned that the devil is attacking you sometimes. What does he do to you?

Strangle me or punch me or tear me with his claws or do whatever he can to hurt me. But that only brings me closer to God, so that is okay. But what he has been doing more recently is, he has been trying to distract me in prayer and being very abusive.

He is saying, "Your prayers don't mean anything, they are worthless, why are you still praying, God doesn't answer your prayers…" I hear this audibly, sometimes in my head.

Or, as I am praying, he will be just talking and talking incessantly, swearing and abusive stuff, trying to stop me.

When I was a little bit sick in Africa this time, I caught a virus, and I was down a bit because I was sick. The evil one was attacking me a lot mentally and audibly, very abusive, about me and my family, the Church and God. I was sick at that time, and after about one week, I just thought I couldn't handle it anymore, when Jesus just said to me, "Just tell Me you love Me." So I started saying it over and over in my mind and within a few minutes, I was in ecstasy, and it was all lifted from me. It was wonderful.

Did the devil identify himself?

He does, he calls himself Lucifer. It is not only the devil, it is evil angels as well that do things, but I try and ignore him. He is defeated, so why bother with him?

When you get tired and you are down, do you ever say, "God, why do You allow this to happen?"

No, not with the attacks. I see them as a way to come closer to God and it also shows me that I am doing the right thing, because if I was not doing the right thing, he wouldn't be attacking me.

For other people who might be attacked in other ways, not physically or verbally, what can be their mindset? What is the positive that can come out of that?

I can only say the positive for me, and hopefully, it will be the same for everyone else. When Lucifer attacks me, I see it as a way of coming closer to God, because the more he attacks me, the more I give myself to God. Even if I think I am about to die, I just give myself to God totally and say, "If it is Your will, I will accept it."

I hope that is how it will be for every person, that the more they are attacked, the more they would turn to God to seek His help, His strength. Also I turn more to the sacraments, because that is where all the power of God comes from in my life, it is the Eucharist, and of course, confession. So, when things get quite intense, I continue going to the Eucharist every day and go to confession five or six times a week, if I can, that is my normal.

Why do you need to go so often?

Because I sin every day. I'm not holy. I am just an average person like anyone else, it is just God doing some things in my life. The reason why I go is, having seen the beauty of God in the Eucharist, having seen God in the Eucharist, every time I receive Jesus, I want to be as pure as I can, and at times, I feel so offensive to Him. The way for me to be pure is to go and confess my sins, so that I can receive Him with a pure heart without hurting Him. When He comes into me, if I have sin, badness within me, that must hurt Him, and I don't want to hurt Him in any way. I know He lowers Himself to come into me, and it is a wonderful grace, so I want to make myself as clean as possible.

I go several times a week because of the work I do and because of the things that happen in that work, there are all sorts of temptations, and sometimes, I slip up quite badly. For me, confession is also strengthening, because it keeps me looking at myself, looking at my weaknesses, seeing how fragile I am, how easily I can be led away from God. Doing this work every day, I have to keep my focus on God by looking at my weaknesses, and then, through that, reaching out to God so that I can get His strength to overcome my weaknesses.

Saint Teresa of Avila put it very plainly for me once, when I was struggling with myself: She said, "In me my weakness, in God my strength." And I always think of that when I struggle.

When you look back at who you used to be, are you amazed at yourself? You are such a different person than that motorcycle gangster you used to be.

I am amazed at the power of God, because it is God's grace that has done everything. All I have done is say yes.I think I would have been stupid not to say yes, because having experienced all the pain and suffering in my life in the past and all of a sudden to have that sweet touch of His love that makes you feel good, I would have been stupid to turn away from that. I think, anyone who would have been touched in that way by God would say yes as I have. So I don't think I am holy, I think I just did what anyone would do, if they had gone through what I have gone through. All I am saying is yes to God, and He does everything else.

But in the very beginning, you didn't say yes straight away.

Yes, I struggled for a while. But it is never too late. My father is a good example. He died on August 21st, 2002. My father was shot down in the Second World War in a plane, and it really affected him badly, and he became alcoholic, violent, all the bad things. Even when they told him he was dying of cancer, he was still drinking a vodka in the morning when he woke up. It was a very bad life.

But I kept praying to God that just He would convert him, and within a few months before his death, he converted completely. He turned to God, embraced God, he spoke about God in ways he would have never spoken about Him before. One of the wonderful blessings was, he wasn't going to have any flowers on his coffin, but right in the last moment, he decided to have a white and a red rose, and, of course, this was a sign of Divine Mercy.

So even someone who was extremely bad, and he was bad, and I understand why, but God forgave him and God welcomed him into His mercy as He will for every person. For me, it was a great example again that even at the last second, it is not too late. And I pray that everyone converts, even if it is at their last breath, because that is not too late.

God tells me He loves everyone, and it doesn't matter what they have done, He wants to forgive them. He just wants to bring people into His love, so that they can live eternally with Him in joy, in happiness. He said in Scriptures that He will forgive sins, and no sin is bigger than God's mercy.

I encourage people: Please, please, turn to God, no matter what you have done, even if you feel you are unworthy, even if you feel you are the worst person in the world, you feel so bad about yourself and angry and bitter with everyone – just turn to God. He loves you, He will be merciful to you, and He will change you for the better. No one is rejected by God, sadly it is people who reject God.

Finally, is there any prayer you want us to pray each day?

"Jesus, I love You." You know, if I say "Jesus, I love You, Jesus, I love You", over and over I will be going into ecstasy.

7   Questions and Answers

What is the Meaning of Suffering?

Suffering can be redemptive. It can bring you closer to God if you can see that you are sharing in God's suffering on the cross, that you are just sharing in a little way and become part of that suffering to try and lift the pain in the world. Then the Lord can use that offering that you give with grace that He will reward you with, to save other people, to help save souls, even to release souls from purgatory. There is so much God can do through suffering if we just accept it in love and offer it back to God rather than feeling sorry for ourselves. See it as a grace that God has given us and use it in the way that God wants us to use it.

So often, as we think of our suffering we feel sorry for ourselves, a self pity. We truly do not understand what suffering is, it can be such a grace when you offer it to Jesus, offer it to Him on the cross. When we do this He takes our suffering deep into His heart to use in saving souls, to bring people back to Him. So suffering is a grace, such a special grace that is offered to many people. So many people do not understand this and all they seem to feel is pity for themselves, "Why is this happening to me? Why am I sick? Why not someone else?" People often ask me - because so many have been healed when I pray over them, and again it is God who heals them, the Father and Jesus and the Holy Spirit, I certainly do not do anything, all I do is I stand there and pray - but they ask, "Well, you have got diabetes. Why didn't the Lord heal you?"

Before the Lord came to me, I used to say that I would give almost anything to get rid of diabetes because it used to inhibit my lifestyle so very much, all the sport I played. After the Lord came to me, He healed me in the way that was best for me, which was spiritually. He healed me in the way I needed to be healed. I still have the diabetes. It means nothing now. It really does not mean anything to me, where before it meant so very much. Now I offer the diabetes and other suffering that I get. I offer it to the Lord for Him to use in the way He wants to help other people and it may be to heal people.

I remember one woman I prayed over and she had a frozen shoulder. I prayed over her and her shoulder was healed straight away. I woke up the next morning with a frozen shoulder. I have had it two years now but I do not ask the Lord to take it from me. He gave it to me for a reason. So I offer it to Him every day and even when I pray over people, my shoulder hurts so very much because it is hard to lift my arm up. I say to the Lord, "You gave this to me for a reason, and if that is what You want, then I return it to You as an offering of love to do with as You want." So suffering can be a grace if you accept it for what it is but it can also be a burden if you do not accept it for what it is, if you just see the sorrow in yourself from the suffering, you are full of self pity, thinking of yourself all the time and not realizing what a grace suffering can be.

Is this a period of mercy?

Well, to me, the period of mercy is endless. Is this a period of judgment? Maybe it is, but it is within the period of mercy, because God's mercy is forever. He offers us forgiveness forever. Right unto the last moment of our life on earth He offers forgiveness, and I think He offers it to everyone up to the last moment.

Also, it is a period of judgment. The Lord is saying to us now, "Look at yourselves." He is giving us so many signs to say, "Look at yourselves, change your lives, look at the sins in your life, change and come closer to Me, live as you are supposed to before it is too late." The Lord has said so often that there is a day of judgment coming. No one knows when it is, I do not profess, too. What the Lord says to me is to tell people, change, start to pray, receive the sacraments, turn back to God, love God, love each other, and when that day of judgment comes, then your heart will be close to God and you will be rewarded by God, not punished.

The warning or the mini judgment that many people are concerned about and some are looking forward to and some are not, in a way the Lord took me through that, I hope I will never have to go through it again, but I am sure I will. The day Jesus came to me, He showed me most of the sins in my life. He showed me His passion on the cross and it truly broke my heart because I saw how my sins had contributed to that. I saw them as the strokes of the whip, as the crown of thorns, as the cross, as the nails, as the spear. I saw my sins contributing to the Lord's suffering on the cross and I saw through my life all He offered me was love, forgiveness, understanding. I just kept seeing how I hurt Jesus, how I had rejected Him over and over, and I kept seeing how sweet He was, how much He loved me, how He gave His life for me, and yet I still rejected Him and did not even think about Him at times.

Then the Lord said, "Through all those times, I was still there by your side, loving you and I am waiting for you to turn to Me and ask for forgiveness." He encouraged me to ask and eventually, when I did, He forgave me my sins, and it was like a weight being taken from my shoulders. What He showed me at that time was that His forgiveness is for everyone. It does not matter what you have done, even if you are the worst person in the world, the Lord offers you forgiveness if you truly repent, if you open your heart and say to God, "I am sorry for what I have done, please forgive me, help me to change." He will forgive, He does love you and He will help you become the person you are created to be.

That is what the mini judgment is. It is showing you yourself, taking away those rose coloured glasses where you only see the goodness in yourself, the good things in your life and thinking how wonderful you are. All of a sudden, the Lord opens your heart, opens your soul and shows you how you have really been living, shows you the sins of your life, shows you how offensive to God they are and when you see that, you do not want to sin anymore.

What happens if we fail to respond to the call of God to change, to become better people, to come closer to God?

Well, then we make our own free choice to accept an eternity of suffering. He will bring us to Heaven if we live as we are supposed to but He also says to people they have a free choice. If people do not want to live that way, even with all the love He is offering them, even with all the guidance He is offering them, even if people deny that, it is not God that is forcing suffering upon them. They are inviting this themselves. These people are saying freely, that they do not want to come to Heaven, that they want to choose hell, and that is their free choice.

What the Lord is saying and through His Blessed Mother so often nowadays is, "Change, pray, receive the sacraments, love each other, do not hurt each other, turn back to God." That is the message, "Come back to God, live in God's love and avoid hell, because if you do not, that is the only place you are going to go."

With a little bit of faith people should turn and say to God, "Help me believe. Lord, I open my heart, help me believe, because I want to come to Heaven, I want to be with You, just help me to understand what You are offering me." Knowing that God is real and He is there offering us His love, His love forever in Heaven.

Are statues and pictures of angels and saints still important today?

Often I see statues in church bleeding and changing and coming to life. It is so wonderful to go into a church and a statue of a saint comes to life and there is the saint before you. The statues of course as we all know were used in early times to represent the saints when we did not have photographs and pictures. People turned to the statues and recognized that saint. Today we seem to be turning away from that, we think we do not need the statues, we think that maybe they are not important now in the church. However, they are because through the saints in the statues we see ways of coming closer to God, we see how they lived and how we should try and live because we should all try to be saints. That is what God created us to be.

So when we see these statues it reminds us of the way these people gave their lives for God, how they devoted their lives to God. When we see the statues of Our Blessed Mother and of Our Lord before us, again, it reminds us in so many different ways of Our Blessed Mother, of what she gave for God, of what she gave for us. How she suffers so much nowadays with the sin that is in the world, how offensive it is to God and because of that how it hurts His Blessed Mother.

Of course, in the statues of Our Lord, when we see His Sacred Heart, it is there saying to us, "I love you and I am offering you My heart." When you see statues where He is suffering, He is saying, "I did this for you because I love you and I am offering you forgiveness. I suffered for you in a personal way, in an individual way because I love you as you are but I want you to change. I want you to come closer to Me, and it does not matter what you have done, I love you so much I will forgive you anything if you just turn and come to Me."

So in these statues that we have, they are showing us many different things, many ways of coming closer to God, many ways that God wants to offer us His love, many ways that He wants to show us that He loves us and wants to forgive us and in many ways it shows His Blessed Mother leading us closer and closer to God, so the statues are very important.

What is the Triumph of the Immaculate Heart?

A wonderful thing. I look forward to the day. It is the day when souls are saved and they come back to God. When Our Blessed Mother leads so many back to the Heart of Jesus, the Father and the Holy Spirit. The triumph of the heart is when evil is defeated in this world, when satan is cast down into hell, when love reigns in this world, when there is no hate, no anger, no sorrow, no suffering, just love of God, living in that love, living and sharing that love with each other, embracing this love in our life completely and not turning away from that as we do today. So the triumph of the Immaculate Heart of Mary is when God's love reigns supreme in this world.

Is the evil worse today than it was years ago?

I think that we have perfected the art of sinning. We have just refined the sins that they had in the past and we are more blatant and more open with it. Sin is accepted more freely where in the past many people stood against sin. Homosexuality used to be hidden away, people did not accept it but now it is out in the open. It still was there in the past but now today we accept the sin more readily and it is the same with many other sins. We accept them and see them as part of life where in the past they were not accepted. So we have become more open to sin and sin is growing. The sin is the same but there is more of it.

Some people have an apocalyptic view, looking at all the tension in today's world. There are so many "messages" from different sources circulating, putting people into fear...

Let me tell you, I do not believe the end times will come in your lifetime nor in my lifetime but no one knows the day. The Lord is telling me not to worry about these things, and He said, people don't understand when messages are given by saints, often they are interpreted by our human mind, not with spiritual sight and so we misinterpret what God is saying to us.

You know, a day in God could be a thousand years for us, so the end times and all these apocalyptic things – people were asking me when I started giving talks in 1994, they were asking if the anti-Christ would come in 1998, and I said, "Don't worry." Then 1998 came, and they were asking about 1999, then about the year 2000, 2001. We are still here and it has not happened.

Many Catholics are more like Jehovah's Witnesses, they keep coming up with these dates. Believe me, God tells me not to worry about the end times, to live today for Him and to take His love to everyone, not to worry about tomorrow. That is in God's hands.

God always warns against the sins, and we have got some terrible sins that are going on, the world is a terrible place, so many bad things are happening. But that doesn't mean the end of the world is coming. No one knows that time, and anybody who professes to know is actually going against Scripture, because Jesus said, no one but the Father know the end times (Mathew 24, 36).Jesus said to the apostles, "Don't worry about tomorrow, worry about today. Live your faith today." And that is the same call for us.

If the end times happen next year, well, that is in God's hands. But I firmly believe in what the Lord is telling me, that it won't happen in my lifetime. We just should be going on in our faith, because this could be a distraction. Many people have been sitting back, saying, we are waiting for God to do something, to do this big sign, to have this mini judgement and they are not doing much themselves. But that is not our faith. Our faith is to get out there to share God's love, and not to do it by fear, that is not the Catholic way. We have to go out in love.

If you bring people back by fear, once they get out of that fear, they don't stay. I noticed that in 1998, when many people had come back to the Church because they thought 1998 would be the time when it all finished – many of them dropped away, because nothing happened. So, fear doesn't get people to stay, it is love that does, and that is what we have to focus on.

Sadly today, there are still many people going round spreading this fear. But the Catholic faith is not one of fear, it is one of love. Sadly, this message has been mixed up somewhere. When you look to what the Pope is saying, what the hierarchy of the Church is saying, the Pope has made several statements now on the end times, telling people not to worry about it, to get on with their faith, this is not the end times. This is the Pope speaking, and I hear people saying, "Isn't this Pope great," and then, the next minute, I hear them saying exactly the opposite of what the Pope is saying. I mean, there is something not quite right here.

Have you seen Our Lord and Our Lady cry?

Yes, I have. I saw Our Lady cry one time. She was pouring tears out on all the babies that are being aborted below her and her tears were just dripping down on these babies. She had her arms open wide, saying, "My children. My babies!" and she was broken hearted to see what we are doing to them, to the babies, to the innocents, the sweet innocents. Heaven looks down upon earth, it sees the sin here, it sees souls that are being taken away from God, the lives that are being prevented from living by the sin of abortion. So many terrible things happening in this world. Heaven looks down and sheds tears at the way we welcome satan with open arms into our lives. Yet when God is there offering us love, we turn away, we do not seem to want the goodness, we do not seem to want love, we turn to the evil, to the badness, because it looks so attractive. That is why Heaven is crying, because we are closing our eyes, we are being blinded to God's love and we are turning down the wrong path. Due to this souls are going to be lost unless they come back to the path of love, the path which is Jesus through His Blessed Mother.

The greatest sin of course is the sin of pride but there are so many sins that pride makes us do. One of the greatest offences to God today is abortion. To see the young babies, before they are even born, killed. It is terrible how we do this. We are killing the next generation, the next priests, nuns, Popes, presidents, doctors...we are just killing them for no reason other than what we feel is important to us. Maybe we need a new car, maybe we need to go on holidays, maybe it is inappropriate to have children around our house, or so we think. So for our pride and our selfishness we kill the children because they are going to impinge on our lifestyle. It is going to affect our lifestyle, maybe we cannot have that extra holiday, so we better not have a child. What value of life is that?

God is the only one who can give or has the right to take life and when we start to put ourselves as the people who can judge who lives or who dies, that is a terrible sin because it is the sin of pride saying that we are on the same level as God, we can judge life. It is only God who can do that, it is only God who can give or has the right to take life and all of a sudden we are saying that we have the right to do that and what an insult that is to God.

What can you say about Priests and religious people?

I have seen Our Blessed Mother and Jesus so concerned at times about what is happening with the religious, with the ordained. Sometimes so happy, seeing such beautiful priests and nuns who are living close to God and reflecting God's love in this world. That is what they are there for, to become an image of God for us, to bring us closer to God but sometimes there are those that maybe get confused and led away and the Lord is very sad at this. So often I hear people condemning priests and saying, "Isn't it terrible, look what this priest has done? This priest is going down the wrong path, he is too liberal."

Instead of doing that, we should be praying for the priests, praying that they be strengthened in the graces and gifts of God, praying that they come closer to God, praying that they understand what God expects of them in this world to bring us closer to Him. So often we condemn them, we judge them and only God has the right to do that. What we should be doing is offering them forgiveness, understanding and love, but frequently we forget that and we are quick to condemn them. If we see a priest on the news or maybe in the newspapers who has done something wrong, we forget about the other 99% of priests that are really good and holy. We only remember the 1% that may have done something wrong. We are so quick to judge those priests and say, "Isn't it terrible, look at those terrible priests." Instead what we have got to understand is that they are human as you and I are and they need love, they need support, they need help. We should not be condemning, we should be forgiving, because Jesus says we must forgive to be forgiven. So we should not hold on to these feelings. We should pray and help these priests and reach out in love to help them come closer to God just as they are meant to help us.

How important is Prayer, Fasting and Sacrifice for the Conversion of the World?

Prayer is one of the most powerful gifts that we have in our hands. It is more powerful than any atomic weapon, than any weapons that we have. Prayer is one of the most powerful gifts God gives us apart from the sacraments. When we pray from our heart and truly believe and trust in God that our prayers will be answered, then they will be. We have got to have trust and belief. When we have doubts, then we are saying, "God, we do not completely trust in you. We do not believe that this is going to happen." Again, that is our free choice but if we can open our hearts and ask from our hearts for the best for other people, God will answer our prayers, He said he will. He will answer them in the way He sees that is best and in the time that He sees as best. So often, people expect it to happen tomorrow. Often it does not work that way, sometimes it does, sometimes it is much later; it is in God's time.

My mother prayed for me for over thirty years but it took more than thirty years before God came to me and changed me but she did not give up. So many people have prayed for the conversion of Russia, for seventy years I think. Many of them did not give up, some did. It took seventy years then Russia was freed from Communism but it did not happen straight away, it happened in God's time. So when we can understand that, our prayers will be answered and in the way and in the time that God wants to answer them, when we open our hearts and believe and trust in Him, then they will be answered.

You were asking about sacrifice. The more that you can sacrifice, the more that you can give in love to God then the more your prayers will be answered, more souls will be saved, more people will come back to God and so many graces will be granted. Sometimes people when they sacrifice, they sacrifice with this little bit of resentment, this feeling of how good they are and they feel it is something special that they are doing. When you feel this way then it is your pride. What you should be saying when you are sacrificing is, "I am giving it to You, God, because I love You and in that love of You I want others to find that love. So I sacrifice this for You, Lord, because I love You so much and I want Your love to touch others." When you do that do not see that you are giving but that you are receiving because when you sacrifice you receive God's love in a special way, in a deeper way. So what we can do, we can pray and pray and trust in our prayers, receive the sacraments. When we receive the sacraments, do not only receive them for ourselves, offer them for other people because there is a grace where we can share our sacraments spiritually. So you can offer the sacraments for other people and they will be shared in some way with them by the grace of God. So it is prayer and a sacramental life and believing and trusting in God, that is what we can do to help overcome sin in this world and defeat evil.

What can you say about the death penalty?

The truth is always the truth. It is only our perception of it that changes and we change our perception of the truth to suit ourselves. So we can make even the worst sins seem okay. Many people today agree with the death penalty. Many Catholics do. How can they? Look at Jesus, look at His life, He said you must not kill. Turn the other cheek, love your enemies, repay evil with kindness. He showed

183

this Himself when He went to the cross. He had the power of Heaven at His disposal but He did not turn it upon anyone and kill them. He went on the cross in forgiving love and that is how we must be, forgiving in love and we must never agree with the death penalty in any form, because when we do, we are disobedient to God. The death penalty is offensive to God and it should be offensive to all those who profess to love Him.

Why does God allow calamities, disasters, wars etc.?

It is not God, it is us living away from God. I always have to smile when people say: Why does God allow these things. God gives us free choice. Sadly, for most of us, the free choice is to be selfish and greedy and because of that in the Third World, people starve. They die of simple diseases that could be cured with inexpensive drugs. Then people talk about wars and why does God allow wars to happen. Well, it is man who causes wars to happen. We are so quick to blame God for our mistakes. God gives us a paradise and encourages us in love to live as we should. In our stupidity we keep ignoring Him. That is why people suffer and die.

There is so much need in the world, yet the people in the West spend as much money on their lawns that it would cost to feed all the poor across the world? There was a report in England that said the 157 wealthiest people in the world have the same wealth as the 2.7 billion poorest and still we blame God! How stupid we are! If we start to live our faith as we are called to, our Christian, Eucharistic faith, each one of us would be sharing with our brothers and sisters in the Third World. When we would see them suffering, we would not just be putting a little amount in

184

the box for them. Our Christian heart would be saying to us, "Give as much as you can!" Most of us just put in a little bit to ease our guilty conscience and still we call ourselves Christian!

So many Christians are worried about the end times, storing food, water and things they might need and worry about what will be happening in the future but for many of the poor in our world today, it is their end times. Yet what are we doing to help them? Most of us do very little except sit back and blame God saying, "Why does He allow this?" Every Catholic and every Christian who does not help the poor to their full extent should be ashamed of themselves. How dare we say: It is God's fault.

God gives us free will. He encourages us all to live well, He tells us in His Commandments how to live well, how not to hurt each other. In our foolishness, we keep rejecting Him and then often we blame God because we do what is wrong.

Some people ask "Why does God not just stop the bad things?" He wants them to stop, but He wants us to learn to stop them ourselves and in that way our very souls, our spirits can grow to be what they are meant to be: ones of love. If all were to live the way God asks, there would be no pain, no hurt, no suffering. We keep rejecting what He wants and so we suffer. It is not God's fault, it is our fault.

What shall we do when there are mistakes in the Church?

The Church is full of sinners and by the grace of God, hopefully we all will be saints. Our Lord came to save sinners and He gives His Church to save sinners. As it is full of sinners, yes, there will be mistakes at times because we are human, we are weak, it is natural that we will fall at times. However when there are mistakes in the Church, we are not called to be angry, what we are called to do is understand is that this Church is filled with the Holy Spirit. Then we should bow in humble obedience to the Holy Spirit praying and offering the Sacraments that any wrongs will be put right. Then the Holy Spirit in His time and in His way, will put things right. What He calls for is us to trust in His divine power. Sadly today, many people see a little wrong in the Church, get angry, get frustrated and leave the Church. Just because they are angry and frustrated and see errors that people might be doing in the Church, this does not stop this Church being the Body of Christ. Jesus gave us this Church with the full knowledge of our weakness and He hopes that unlike those in John 6, people will not turn their backs and turn away because they do not understand the mystery of this Church and because they are looking with human eyes and human weaknesses.

In the morals and teachings of the Church that are given by Our Lord Jesus through the Apostles and the Popes and the tradition that they carry on, there are no errors. There might be a misunderstanding from us because we look with human eyes rather than asking the Holy Spirit to help us see with spiritual eyes.

Just because the world says it is okay to take things like the oral contraception or it may be okay to kill people at times, this does not make it right. Sadly today, many Catholics just want to blend in with the world and what everyone else accepts. They see the Church as a democracy that should suit them. The Church is not a democracy, if it was a democracy, then It would be the people's church, not

God's Church. This is God's church and not a democracy, it is a Theocracy which is far greater. In true love of God people would want to be obedient to His teachings. In love of self, in pride and in the world, people instead want to turn away from God. This Church is God's, it is His Body, and we can be part of His Body by humbly bowing to His will in the Church and trusting completely in God to guide us along the right path.

For Charismatics, how can they get more gifts or strengthen their gifts?

The answer should be obvious to every one of you. All you need to do is come to the Eucharist, bow down before your Lord humbly, offer yourself totally to Him as an empty vessel and allow Him to fill you with Himself and His Holy Spirit. Then you will find your gifts will explode beyond your wildest dreams because now you will have the power of God, the power of Heaven with you and God will use you to magnify that power. First to magnify that power, you have to come and make yourself small before Him, saying, "Here I am, Lord," in every Eucharist. "Here I am Lord, I have come to do Your will, to serve You." Also when you leave the church, be prepared to take Our Lord Jesus with you wherever you go, sharing Him with everyone unafraid because that is your duty. That is an essential part of your faith. That is the commandment that Jesus gave you to share Him with the world.

Our God is the living God. Our faith is and must be the living faith. That means we do not only live it in the church but we live it every second of our life. It is when we do that, the life of Christ in us will reach out and bring others to life in Him. This is our Eucharistic faith that Jesus Christ Our Lord gave to us and we must truly start to live it if we want the world to change.

The call today from Our Lord Jesus to each one of you is the same today that it was 2000 years ago: Live in obedience to His will, live in Him and be unafraid of taking Him to the world. Until you start to do that, I wonder can you truly call yourself a Catholic.

What can we do about others who go to receive Communion without having been to confession?

We have to encourage people to go to Confession because we should not go to receive Jesus knowing we have serious sin on our souls. So, if I can get to Confession before communion, I try my best to do so because I feel it hurts Jesus to receive Him with sin on my soul and personally, I do not want to hurt Jesus in any way. With others, who are we to judge them? Who are we to say if someone has been to Confession or not? Who are we to say what someone else's relationship with God is? In Scripture, when they brought the adulterous woman to Jesus, He said to the Jews and to the Pharisees "You who are without sin cast the first stone." (John 8, 7). Those Jews were wise enough to see that they all had sin and no one cast a stone. Sadly, so many of us Catholics cannot see our own sin and we quickly cast the first stone.

I am worried about my children who don't attend Church at all and are trapped in materialism.

What you have to do with those fears, first of all give them to Jesus and trust in Him. If you offer your prayers to Him in love of your children and trying to serve Him in your life as best as you can, Jesus will take care of your family. It may not be in the way or time that you see, it may be after you have died but Jesus has said He will answer our prayers when they are for goodness and for love. Surely our prayers for our children, for our family, for our friends are that and Jesus does not break His promises. All He calls for, is us to persevere and to believe that He will answer our prayers.

What if I am not a Catholic but a Christian? Is salvation also possible for me?

God loves Jews, Hindus, Muslims, Catholics, Protestants, Greek-Orthodox, Russian-Orthodox, Serbian Orthodox, everyone. He loves us all the same. Heaven is not for Catholics alone there are going be a lot of other people there because it is what is on your heart that is important. God looks at your heart, how much you know of Him and in that knowledge how much you love Him and how much you're doing for His love. So, if you are not Catholic, it does not mean you are not going to Heaven.

However, I have to say to you, when Jesus came to me, if He had said to me be a Jew, be a Greek, be a Hindu, be a Protestant, that is what I would have been but He did not. He said to me to be a Catholic. He said, "This is the true faith, the faith I gave to Peter." He said, "All the other Christian faiths after that are because of people's disagreements, arguments amongst people."

The Church that God gave is the Catholic Church, it is the true faith, and we must never be ashamed or embarrassed of that but it does not mean God does not love the other people as well and they will not go to Heaven. However the true faith, the one Jesus gave is clearly there in Scripture and it is the Catholic faith.

Why do you think He sent Saint Peter to Rome? Why do you think He sent Saint Paul to Rome? To say to us that Rome is the centre of His Church, this is where He wanted it to be. Why did so many martyrs shed their blood in Rome? Again in them God is saying over and over Rome must be the centre of the Church.

Now I do not know the reason why, but it is His reason. He tells me that the Roman Catholic Church and those churches in obedience to it have the true faith but again that does not mean the others will not be going to Heaven many will. Just as unfortunately many Catholics may not be.

Can one be a true Catholic and a free mason at the same time?

There is a bit of misunderstanding here by people who become masons because when they join the masons many see that they are doing good charitable works and they think, well that is what we are getting into a charitable organization. I have met many masons and I have met 33rd level masons which are very high masons. When they get to those levels and when they get to lower levels, some of the ceremonies they have to do are things like stamping on an imitation of the crown of the Pope and giving insults to God by accepting other Gods and accepting that Lucifer is the brother of The Lord Jesus. Other ceremonies involve placing allegiance to the Masons before allegiance to Our Lord Jesus. Some ceremonies also are almost identical, if not the same, as ceremonies of the satanic churches. At Masonic temples, you will see satanic symbols and they keep bones of the dead there which are used for some of their unchristian activities. Well, in truth, you cannot be a mason and a Catholic. Any Catholic who is a mason should leave the masons immediately.

If you were to ask a full blooded mason, who is a Catholic and who has been in it for a long time, when they die and go to the gates of Heaven and Saint Peter is there asking, "Why should I let you into Heaven?" What would they answer, "Because I am a mason or because I am a Catholic." A mason usually says, "Because I am a mason." In itself, that shows you that Masonry goes completely against Catholicism and truly is not Christian, and no Catholic should be a mason.

Why do the Catholics attach so much importance to Mary?

I just would like to say about our Blessed Mother: First, with your own mother, if people reject your mother, if they say bad things about your mother, and turn away from your mother when she reaches out to offer them help and love, Wouldn't you feel angry towards those people? Wouldn't you be upset with those people? How do you think Jesus feels when people say bad things about His mother, when people reject His mother and turn away from His mother? Surely, that makes Jesus feel unhappy with that person.

You also have to remember: The fact that she was the mother of Jesus, the mother of God, lifts her above any human that ever was or ever will be created. No one else has been in that position, except mother Mary. God chose Mary especially for that. Now if God chose Mary for that and if God called Mary blessed, God called Mary His mother, then why are we turning away from her, why are we rejecting her? In doing so we reject what God has chosen and so we reject the will of God.

Would you like to share some of your experiences with Mary?

Our Blessed Mother stresses over and over, "God first in all things." She is there in times of trouble and when so many things happened to me from the other side, Our Blessed Mother is often there to comfort me and help me through difficult times.

Our Blessed Mother, she truly is our mother. She just loves us and loves us with such a pure love. What a wonderful, wonderful gift God has given us in Mary. She longs for every person in this world to come to the Father and Jesus and the Holy Spirit. She does everything she can, she calls in so many ways to bring the world back to God because she does not want to see anyone suffer, she does not want to see anyone hurt. Our Blessed Mother keeps saying over and over in her messages that the reason we are hurting in this world is because we are living away from God. She is saying, "Come back to God, live with God, live in God, and then you will live a happy life and this world will be a paradise." It is just up to us to make the choice and come to God.

She keeps telling us over and over what is good for us, like mothers do. When mothers see children hurting themselves, mothers say, "Do not do that, that is wrong and it will hurt you." This is what Our Blessed Mother does, now she says to us, "Do not sin, this is wrong, you are hurting yourself when you are doing that. Come and live this way, live this way and be happy and do not be hurt." She truly is our mother and her heart breaks every time she sees someone who offends God, someone who sins, someone who hurts themselves and the people around them. It really hurts our Mother.

Today, many people claim to have visions and locutions. How do these claims strike you in relation to what God has been teaching you on a life of holiness and what He expects from us and the future?

The Lord says to me that He does give messages to many people and He has been throughout the history of the Church and even in the Old Testament, at the time of Elijah, they called the prophets together and there was many of them; more than one. However, what the Lord says is you have to be very careful. If anything contradicts Holy Scripture or the teaching of the Catholic Church, it has to be wrong. So you should check any messages that you are reading from anyone, including mine, and see if they contradict Scripture or Catholic teaching. If they do, then they are wrong and we should not take any notice of them.

The sad thing that I see around the world is that many Catholics are reading various things that are obviously wrong because they go against Holy Scripture and Church teaching and they seem to be blinded to it. I encourage those people as God always encourages me, always refer to Scripture, always refer to Catholic teaching and if it agrees with that, it is right and then it will be from God. If it does not, well it is not from God.

The message God gives me again is not to be afraid of anything. Today many people are frightened of the end times, that the world is going to end in a few years time but this is a big deception. Again satan is working on our fears to close our heart a little bit to what we should be doing. We should be opening our heart to living in the love of God and sharing it with other people but as we think about the end times we start to focus on ourselves, Are we going to die? Our friends or families, are we going to have problems? We have got to store food up and other things for us…self-centered! When you are self-centered God is second. So what satan does today with these things, he gets you to focus on yourself and then you do not live your faith.

If you do store food up and water or whatever and there is a disaster, as a Catholic, as a Christian, you have to share that with other people in need, so it is not going to last you long anyway. If you do not share it, people will know you have this food in there and they may kill you and take it, so what is the point of storing it?

With the Jews in the desert, when they were in need, God gave them the bread, the manna from Heaven. He gave them water from a stone, He gave them the fowl, the meat they needed. Do you think God loves us less than He loved them? He loves us the same, He will give us all that we need. What He tells us in Holy Scripture is, "Seek you first the kingdom of God and everything else will be given unto you." (Mathew 6, 33 and Luke 12, 31). Do not become self-centered, do not start to worry about what is going to happen in the future.

Today, many people are concerned about those end times and as I said, they start to focus on themselves, but in the Third World today, there are people starving. There are people dying from simple diseases that could be cured for a few dollars, a few dollars for medicine which they just do not have and today we forget these people. We look and wonder what is going to happen to us in three or four years' time. Are we going to die? Is the world going to come to an end? For these people in the Third World, this is the end times. They are living the end times now. How dare we be thinking of ourselves, that is totally unchristian. A Christian and Catholic life is to look to your brothers and sisters and take the love of God to them, to share with them, to care for them, to look after them. Yet many of us are focussing on what is going to happen to us in two, five, ten, twenty years' time.

We are not living a Christian life, we are closing our hearts to what we should be doing. This is so wrong, yet we are so blind to it. A Christian life means that we should be worried about the Third World, we should be caring for these people and not worry about ourselves. So do not worry about the end times, live your faith today! This is what Jesus said in Scripture.

Matthew 6:25 "Therefore I tell you, do not worry about your life, what you will eat or drink or about your body."

He said no one knows the end times except the Father, so anyone who says they know the end times today is going against Holy Scripture, it must be wrong. He said to the apostles when they asked Him about the end times, do not worry about tomorrow (Mathew 6, 34), worry about today, about living your faith today, and He calls to us to do the same. So, when you refer to Scripture, you can see where things are obviously wrong. You just have to take time to look. See, are things making you God-centered or are things making you self-centered? If it is self-centered, it is not from God at all, it is from the other one who uses fear, who uses clever tactics to try and distract you.

Today, many people are waiting for a sign, a wonderful thing to happen, that maybe the sun will fall from the sky and then everyone will wake up to God. However, in Fatima, the sun fell from the sky and did the world change much? There are many people now trying to live the Fatima message and praying as Our Lady asked but in general the world took little notice. Maybe the reason was that Catholics did not take the message to the world. They did not live the faith and live the message.

If there is going to be a sign within the next few years which there well may be or there may not be, if it happens and people are not aware of God's love, when this sign happens, many of them will take no notice. What God is calling us to do is to go out and spread His good news, His love, so that if something like this does happen, then people will know to turn to God and be aware of God. That is our duty. Not to sit there and wait for God to do everything, He calls us as He has throughout history to take part in the conversion of sinners, the salvation of souls. He has always called mankind to share in His love in that way but today again, we are going back in the old ways of letting God do it all, of waiting for God to do it all. We have got to play our part. Our part is living the faith, taking it to the world and sharing and caring with others and not being afraid for ourselves, not being self-centered, instead living a God-centered life.

Have you got messages concerning this particular Pope you mentioned?

Yes, I have. Some of them cannot be published, a couple of them are coming up in some future books. Our Lord and Our Blessed Mother always tell me how wonderful this Pope is and how holy he is and what a reflection he is of God's love, a true reflection…always forgiving, always kind, always understanding, always loving and always standing firmly in the truth. Jesus has said many times if we can all try and live as the Pope does, to live as an image of God's love in that way, then we will all be holy and we will all be called to sainthood.

Can you say a little about your bishop and the letters of support from other bishops and priests? And who is your spiritual director?

What happened was when Jesus first came to me, He said to go and see the archbishop. I thought, "How am I going

197

to see him? I am just an average man in the street, he is so busy, he is not going to see me." The Lord insisted, "Go see him, you are going to get to see him." Anyway, through a series of miraculous events I got to see the archbishop and spent some time with him, and he gave me permission to go and carry on doing what God had asked me to do.

I had made the promise to Our Blessed Mother before I went in there, that if the archbishop said, "Well, you stop this and it is not to go on any further," that is what I was doing at that moment, because the saints and Our Blessed Mother had called me to a total obedience to the Catholic Church without question, unless it goes against faith and morals, so I try and live to that. So, if the archbishop had said stop, I would have stopped immediately, and that is still true today, if he tells me to stop tomorrow, I will stop tomorrow.

But in his wisdom, he encouraged me to go out to the world with the message that Jesus was giving me of love, and he appointed a spiritual director, Fr. Gerard Dickinson who was very sceptical. That was a very wise move by the archbishop to appoint a sceptical priest to be the spiritual director, someone who really did not believe in me. After a while, Fr. Gerard had a complete change of heart and has made several statements. He says he completely believes that Our Lord, Our Blessed Mother and the angels and saints are using me. I remain completely obedient to him and to my archbishop. Anything the Church asks me to do, I do, unless it goes against faith and morals, of course because God has told me I must be completely obedient to the Church. Everything I get is given to my spiritual director. I tell him all the things that happen and we discuss them and he is aware of everything even all the personal things and everything that happens in my life.

God tells me that is the way it should be and again He is stressing that I am to have a complete openness so that my spiritual director can guide me properly. So, I hide nothing from him.

Being obedient to the Catholic Church is what God calls everyone to be. I think anyone who has been receiving messages from the Lord must be called to this obedience because the Church is His Body and is filled with His Holy Spirit, so then God would call you to obedience to His Church. Otherwise I do not think you could be receiving messages from Our Lord. So, my archbishop continues to support me as Fr. Dickinson did until he died. The archbishop then appointed Fr. Richard Rustaukaus to be my spiritual director.

The writings have been scrutinized by several theologians, they cannot find anything wrong with them. There have been statements made by Fr. Richard McSorley who is a theologian in Georgestown in America, very well known in the USA and other places, who said, the writings are the best treatise of a mariologist he has ever read in his life. For me, that was wonderful to hear. Several other theologians have made very similar statements. So, the Lord tells me as long as I continue to be obedient to the Church and give everything to the Church, that will help guarantee that mistakes will not happen.

What do you read?

All I read is Holy Scripture. The Lord gives me sometimes a psalm or a few lines every day from Holy Scripture which He helps me understand through the power of the Holy Spirit, who opens that Scripture up to me. He tells me to tell everyone to read Scripture and before they start reading it, to ask the Holy Spirit to show them what God is saying in this Scripture, otherwise we put our human interpretation into it. So Scripture is all I read and daily newspapers…I read them, but otherwise I do not read anything.

Why did you become a Catholic and what about the other Christian churches?

What the Lord explained to me was that the fullness of His truth was in Catholicism. That the fullness of the word of God was in Catholicism, that some of it was in the other Churches, but not in its completeness. I did some research on the other Churches just to find out a little bit about them as the Lord was telling me so much. Interestingly, I discovered that Henry VIII who founded the Anglican Church was buried a Catholic. He refused being buried a Protestant. Maybe he recognised that in the protestant church something was missing.

The other thing the Lord said to me was that Jesus gave us the Catholic Church. You can trace this back to Jesus Himself, all the way. The history of the Catholic Church goes completely to Jesus and follows everything He said. So the Catholic Church was founded by Our Lord Jesus. When I looked to the other Churches and I looked to their history, I saw that every one of them was founded by a man. Jesus said to me, "Whom do you want to follow? Do you want to follow Me or do you want to follow a man who has some belief in what I said or maybe some understanding of it but not a complete understanding not a complete belief. Do you want to follow him or do you want to follow God in the fullness of Divine truth?" The choice to me was obvious…Follow Our Lord Jesus and the fullness of His truth, because man can get confused.

After your conversion, did you stop watching TV or going out etc.?

I enjoy much of the world, I watch TV and I watch movies, but you can do that and still offer those moments to God. I am very careful in what I watch and what I do, but I live a normal life. When I go home, my wife and myself, we go to restaurants, we got to the movies, we go bowling, we do all sorts of things. God does not mind. He is happy when I am enjoying myself, that is what He wants. He wants everyone to enjoy life in goodness and in love.

Did you experience dry times in prayer in order to be purified?

The dryness I have experienced may be a little different from the dryness other people experience. I see the dryness as a way of coming closer to God. Every time I experience dryness, I thank God for it and I ask Him to give me more if that is what He wants and I find that I seem to grow stronger through that. Every one gets dry times and I think it is very sad that so many people in the dry times start to think they have done something wrong or they are really bad and of course, that is generally not true. Some people in those dry times get angry with God and how satan laughs because that is a weakness of faith. The dry times should be seen for what they are. They are graces being given so that we can show the depth of our love to God. Anyone in the good times can say they love God and show love of God. It is when you do so in those difficult moments, you really show you love God. What a gift God gives us, giving us those times where we can show our love for Him.

What are you thinking about what is happening in the Middle East, the tension with Iraq and in Israel etc.?

Jesus told me the other day, and for me, it is quite profound, "I am the prince of peace, I am not the prince of war." The prince of war comes from down below. So, if you are Christian, you should be pacifist, because that is what Jesus was.

Revenge killing is wrong. War is wrong. The moment we seek revenge, the instant we set about to kill our enemy – even in the name of war – we are no different from the terrorists. If we kill people – any people – we, too, are murderers. No exception. God's commandment that thou shalt not kill does not have such a caveat. It does not say, thou shalt not kill – except in times of war. It says, thou shalt not kill, period.

Jesus tells me the correct Christian response is to track down the perpetrators and bring them to justice – according to the rule of law. This is the only way, for it is God's way. There lies before us the heroic opportunity to forgive. One mustn't sacrifice his own soul for the sake of revenge. No Christian should consider revenge as an option. Bombs will not stop evil, they will only fuel it.

What did God tell you about September 11th?

He told me we have to forgive the people who did it, that is the Christian way, no matter what people do. We must not accept what they do, because it is not right, but we have to pray and understand why they did these things, and we have to forgive them. We have to try in love to change the hearts of the Moslem people, the Arab people, because if you try and change them by force, it never works. When in history, if you changed people's hearts by force, did it ever work?

8   Invitation or Advice

For those of you who have read this book and maybe have been touched in some way and you are wondering: What should you do now? Well, the first thing I encourage you to do is go and sit in the church quietly. Just by yourself, close your eyes, sit there quietly and let the Lord touch you, guide you and lead you into what He wants you to do. So often we try and think what we should do and we place our will into our lives. Instead if we just let God guide us, He will guide us into goodness, He will bring us to what is best for us. It is so important that we go to the Church and look for guidance because it is God's Body; it is filled with His Holy Spirit.

In the Church, He can give us all that we need. He can bring us closer to Him and help us to lead a true life, a good life, a happy life, a peaceful life. So the message I would like to give to people today is   if you are not going to church, start going, because since I started going to church, my life has changed so much. It has become joy-filled.

If you are going to church already, I encourage you from a once-a-week person going to Sunday Mass, maybe start going a little more because the more you go to the sacraments, the closer you will come to God, the stronger you will be filled with His love, His graces and gifts and your life and the life of the people around you, your family, your friends, will change. They will change for the better because God will work through you, as you receive Him in the sacraments, He will work through you to change the people around you and to change yourself for the better because that is what God does. He brings His goodness into our life because God is goodness.

If you are going to church regularly, if you are going to Mass often and Confession often, maybe going to prayer groups, I encourage you to spend a little time and think: Are you doing God's will in your life or are you doing you own? So often today, we do our own. I am guilty of that but what I find is that if I sit quietly with God, He guides me, He leads me. Then if I do what He wants every thing works out perfectly. It is when I do what I want, I seem to have problems, I seem to make mistakes. If you look to God, if you sit quietly, ask the Holy Spirit to show you what He wants, just spend time alone, empty your mind and let Him give you the message that He wants to. You will be surprised what you hear. It might not be what you want to hear, but it will be the best thing for you. So turn to God, follow His will, live in His will and share His love with everyone you meet. God bless you all.